IAN R MITCHELL was born in Aberdeen, spen~~~~
Kincorth. He graduated in History from Abe~~~~
a couple of years working as a paper mill labo~~~~ ~~~~gineering machinist, and
subsequently moved to Glasgow. Ian taught History at Clydebank College for
over 20 years and whilst there wrote a standard textbook on *Bismarck and the
Development of Germany*. He has written several books on mountaineering
including the classic *Mountain Days & Bothy Nights* (1987), and *A View from the
Ridge* (1991) (both co-authored with Dave Brown), the latter of which won the
Boardman-Tasker Prize for Mountain Literature. More recently he has developed
an interest in urban heritage and walking, and the recent fruits of this were *This
City Now: Glasgow and its Working Class Past* (2005) and *Clydeside: Red,
Orange and Green* (2009).

*Mitchell has honoured the spirit of [Aberdeen's] fine,
hard-working people with a splendid book.*
THE PRESS AND JOURNAL

*So is Ian Mitchell's psychogeographical, intermittently
autobiographical, seven-fold daunder beyond and behind
the silver city's glitz and glitter a worthy addition to the...
books about Aberdeen? I think it is.*
NORTHWORDS NOW

Other books by Ian R Mitchell

Non-Fiction

Mountain Days & Bothy Nights (1987) with Dave Brown

A View from the Ridge (1991, re-issued 2007) also with Dave Brown

Scotland's Mountains before the Mountaineers (1998)

On the Trail of Queen Victoria in the Highlands (2001)

Walking through Scotland's History (2000, re-issued 2007)

This City Now: Glasgow and its Working Class Past (2005)

Clydeside: Red, Orange and Green (2009)

Fiction

Mountain Outlaw: Ewan MacPhee (2003)

Winter in Berlin, or The Mitropa Smile (2009)

Aberdeen Beyond the Granite

IAN R MITCHELL

Luath Press Limited

EDINBURGH

www.luath.co.uk

First published 2010
Reprinted 2011
Reprinted 2013
Reprinted 2015

ISBN: 978-1-906817-22-0

The paper used in this book is recyclable. It is made from
low chlorine pulps produced in a low energy, low emissions manner
from renewable forests.

Printed and bound by
Bell & Bain Ltd., Glasgow

Typeset in 11 point Sabon
by 3btype.com

Contents

Foreword   John Aberdein   7

Acknowledgements   9

Maps   10

Introduction   *Aberdeen 1800–2000*   15

PLACES

CHAPTER ONE   Hairbouring Regrets?   33

CHAPTER TWO   Owir the Watter   43

CHAPTER THREE   Fit Wye tae Fittie?   57

CHAPTER FOUR   The Grunnit Hairt of the Granite City   67

CHAPTER FIVE   Haudagain tae Kittybrewster   81

CHAPTER SIX   Roon Aboot Rosemount   93

CHAPTER SEVEN   Kincorth: Nithing bit Hooses?   103

PEOPLE

CHAPTER EIGHT   Willie Thom: The Weaver Bard of Bon Accord   113

CHAPTER NINE   *Proletarian Pilgrimage*: A Forgotten Classic   123

CHAPTER TEN   The Other Name on the Everest Memorial: Alexander Kellas, Himalayan Pioneer   135

CHAPTER ELEVEN   The Names on the Slugain Howff Memorial: The Dreamers of Beinn a' Bhuird   145

Foreword

I LIKE THIS BOOK. There is something fine and staunch about it. At such a pivotal point in the North East's destiny, besieged as it is by schemes for yet mair malls and Ready-Mix plazas, not to mention pitch 'n' putt complexes straight out of *Kubla Khan*, Ian Mitchell takes a warm, provocative, dander through the core of the city, the beating heart of its working class ancestry, and the spirit of its pioneers. If there is a thesis in this set of essays, it is that the city and its hinterland have a lot to draw strength from, much to grip fast to – and that the glaikit, greed-driven, Gadarene scramble of recent years has to be brought under control.

In many ways, I suppose, Ian Mitchell's call in this volume parallels the apocalyptic vision of my tragi-comic *Strip the Willow* (2009), an Aberdeen/Uberdeen novel which dramatises the descent of a moneyed tycoon on a bankrupt city, and the muckle havoc thereby wreaked. Drafted as prophecy a couple of years back, *Strip the Willow* seems to become eerily truer by the day.

So it's no surprise that I find so much that is sympathetic in Ian Mitchell. He is wide-ranging, sharp, knowledgeable and downright funny. For example, he goes on a visit to stark East Germany before the Berlin Wall comes down only to discover, 'The GDR was like being back in Kincorth a quarter of a century before.' Of course even that turns out to be relative, for as an actual inhabitant of Kincorth in that era, he recalls how coming down to the Constitution Street area in the 1960s was 'like entering bandit territory.' That was *my* area, thanks Ian! Or he'll swing with ease through history and recount how 'exiled revolutionaries, such as the aged anarchist thinker Kropotkin, who were returning to Russia, departed from Aberdeen, and representatives of the new Bolshevik government on occasion used the city as their entry point to Britain.' Big references thus jostle with the small change of nostalgia.

Walk with him through history, walk with him through the solid working districts of Torry, Fittie and Woodside. The rusty trawlers, the tight communities, the underpaying mills. But not *tight* in that sense. He makes the interesting point, and I agree with him, that the alleged meanness of Aberdonians was largely the desire to survive decently, to *manage*, to keep one's head up, in tough times, on extremely limited means. Walk with him, therefore, as he mixes social anger and antiquarian delight, pride and scunneration.

'It is dangerous to make categorical statements, but here is one,' says Ian Mitchell. 'There has been scarcely a single building of architectural merit or originality put up in this city for many decades; oil money has disfigured, not transfigured, Aberdeen.'

But he praises the Castlegate, with its 'hinge' at Archibald Simpson's, and he praises the preservation of the gilt Parthenon frieze in its converted pub. He calls for a new breed of statues to be commissioned, to dot and dignify the town: and it is clear what characters he'd be glad to see chiselled and celebrated: the likes of the weaver-bard, Willie Thom, a proletarian memoirist like John Paton, who dedicated his work to Lewis Grassic Gibbon, and outstanding mountaineers like Alexander Kellas and Tom Patey.

For indeed one of the most resonant themes in Ian Mitchell's philosophy is that Aberdeen's hinterland goes significantly beyond the weel-kent farmlands of Buchan, Donside, Deeside and the Mearns. The Cairngorms form a massive background, an abiding source of challenge and comradeship, where – transcending economic trammels – new routes can aye be forged.

New routes – or the joys of recognition – however minded, you can take your fill here.

John Aberdein

Acknowledgements

TWO PEOPLE WERE INADVERTENTLY at least partially responsible for this book. Paul Dukes lamented that there was no book like my Glasgow work, *This City Now*, on Aberdeen, and Lorna Dey suggested it was time I 're-connected with the whole North East experience'. *Fowk should mebbi be mair canny fit they say.*

Mike Dey's forensic examination of the draft manuscript removed a number of inaccuracies and misjudgements, but none of us are perfect, so any such that remain overlooked are entirely my responsibility. Mike also gave me a wee *shoudie* in the direction of a less detached approach to my task, which led me towards an almost cathartic re-engagement with Aberdeen that I had not anticipated when I began to write. Ashie Brebner and Chesty Bruce provided comments on the chapter on Slugain Howff and Beinn a' Bhuird and also on chapters three and four, relating to where they grew up in Grunnit Hairt and Fittie.

All visual material reproduced in this book is from public domain sources unless otherwise stated. Most of the textual material in this book consists of the re-working and further development of material which I have already had published elsewhere, viz. *History Scotland*, *Scots Magazine* and the *Scottish Mountaineering Club Journal*. But just in case readers think *it's aa cauld kale hettit up*, the chapters on the Harbour and Kincorth are completely new.

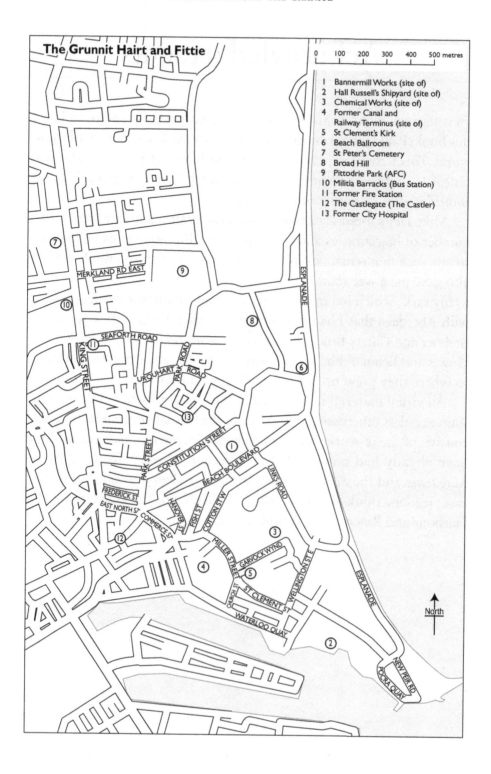

The Grunnit Hairt and Fittie

0   100   200   300   400   500 metres

1 Bannermill Works (site of)
2 Hall Russell's Shipyard (site of)
3 Chemical Works (site of)
4 Former Canal and
   Railway Terminus (site of)
5 St Clement's Kirk
6 Beach Ballroom
7 St Peter's Cemetery
8 Broad Hill
9 Pittodrie Park (AFC)
10 Militia Barracks (Bus Station)
11 Former Fire Station
12 The Castlegate (The Castler)
13 Former City Hospital

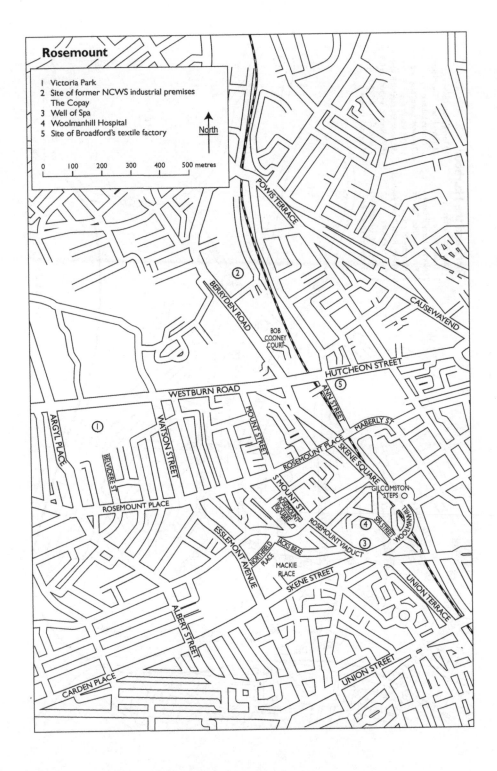

Rosemount

1 Victoria Park
2 Site of former NCWS industrial premises
   The Copay
3 Well of Spa
4 Woolmanhill Hospital
5 Site of Broadford's textile factory

North

0   100   200   300   400   500 metres

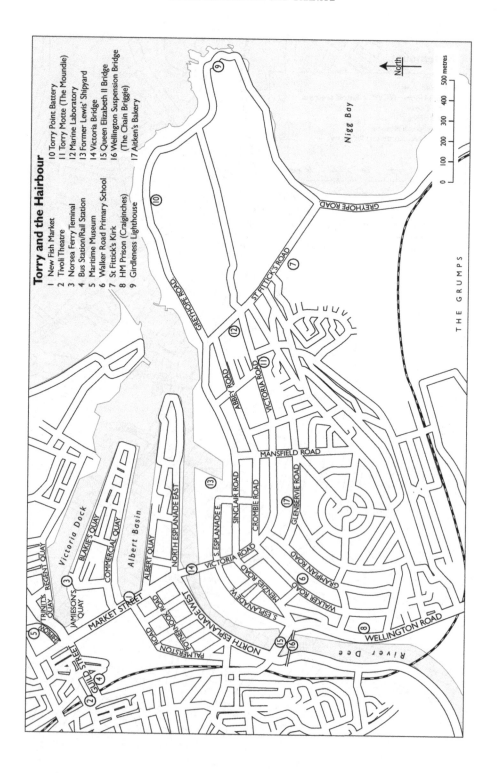

Torry and the Hairbour

1 New Fish Market
2 Tivoli Theatre
3 Norsea Ferry Terminal
4 Bus Station/Rail Station
5 Maritime Museum
6 Walker Road Primary School
7 St Fittick's Kirk
8 HM Prison (Craiginches)
9 Girdleness Lighthouse
10 Torry Point Battery
11 Torry Motte (The Moundie)
12 Marine Laboratory
13 Former Lewis' Shipyard
14 Victoria Bridge
15 Queen Elizabeth II Bridge
16 Wellington Suspension Bridge
   (The Chain Briggie)
17 Aitken's Bakery

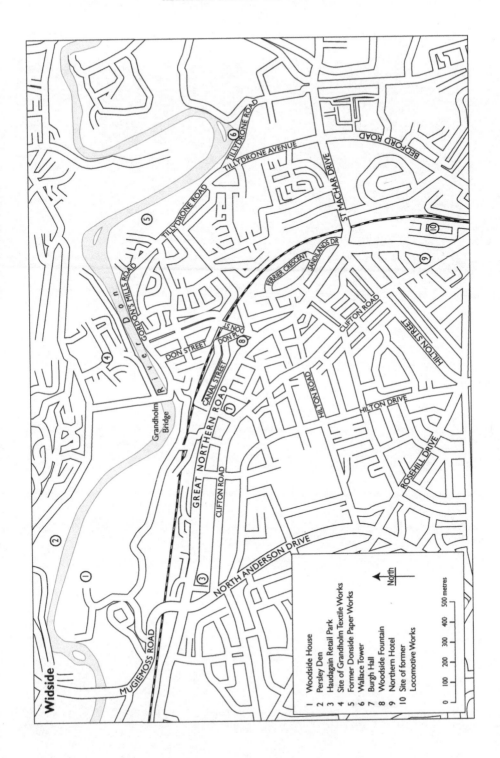

Widside

Key:
1 — Woodside House
2 — Persley Den
3 — Haudagain Retail Park
4 — Site of Grandholm Textile Works
5 — Former Donside Paper Works
6 — Wallace Tower
7 — Burgh Hall
8 — Woodside Fountain
9 — Northern Hotel
10 — Site of former Locomotive Works

0 100 200 300 400 500 metres

Introduction

Aberdeen 1800–2000

THE INHABITANTS OF ABERDEEN have a patriotism that few similar-sized cities can match; most of its indwellers would probably agree that 'the toun and twal mile roun', to borrow a local phrase, is as near to heaven as it gets on this earth. Non-academic writing in the form of local history about the city tends to reflect this and generally displays the quiet self-satisfaction of the *'Wha's* (or *Fa's) like us?'* genre. By and large Aberdonians are happy to see themselves as they see themselves, not 'as ithers see them'.[1] To outsiders in contrast Aberdeen is often an underloved city. Modern travel writers like Theroux and Bryson, those celebrity one-stop-shopping modern explorers, have savaged the place and its people based on a totally inadequate acquaintance. But even the nearby-born and temporary resident of Aberdeen Lewis Grassic Gibbon gave a not wholly flattering picture of the Granite City in the book *Scottish Scene,* which he co-authored with Hugh MacDiarmid in the 1930s.

Though he described Aberdeen as 'exasperatingly lovable' (a statement I would agree with) and talked of the 'glowing wonder' of its granite buildings, 'shining with fine flame, cold and amber and gold', Gibbon also wrote:

> Bleakness, not meanness or jollity is the keynote to the Aberdeen character... Aberdeen is the cleanest city in Britain: it makes you long for good, wholesome dirt... Union Street has as much warmth in its face as a dowager duchess asked to contribute to the Red International relief... [Gibbon further describes] the thin Aberdonian voice in the thin local patois... the flinty cliffs of Union Street, the flinty cheeks and disharmonic faces that press about you in an Aberdeen tram.

Outsiders often experience Aberdeen as close and clannish and find it difficult to integrate. Many non-natives also feel the climate, like the people, is cold, and they do not respond to the steely granite architecture, sparkling and lovely in sunshine, but dreary in the rain. Few of the oil boom immigrants of the last 30 years have settled in the city, either moving out to the countryside into middle class Sowetos like Westhill or moving on when their employment ended. (Indeed, in the '80s and '90s two-thirds of those working in oil were not permanent residents of the North East, but commuters or transient workers.) But for those who accept Aberdeen for what it is – variously described as the largest village in the world or more favourably as the most perfect provincial city in the UK – it is a hugely intriguing place with a unique character, as unique as the granite from which it has been built. And it is where I was born.

It was TS Eliot (whom I am certain never visited Aberdeen) who commented that all our travelling is to arrive back at the place from which we started and to know it for the first time. He may have been talking metaphorically about life as a journey, but his statement is also true of physical places. Bred in Aberdeen, I left the town in my mid-20s and have been away from it for many more years than I spent there. I can certainly echo Eliot's words and I feel that repeated visits – often several times a year in the last four decades or so – with the benefit of an outsider's perspective have made me begin to understand things I only partially glimpsed about the place before. A recent book about Aberdeen has added enormously to this understanding, and while reading it my brain echoed to the sound of penny after penny dropping. Things I took as given now became explained and connected, and things unsuspected were revealed. This book, *Aberdeen 1800–2000: A New History* (edited by WH Fraser and Clive H Lee, published by Tuckwell Press), should be a starting point for all who want to understand the city. Here follow a few thoughts stimulated by the volume (based on the extensive re-working of a review of the work I wrote when it first appeared in 2000), which as a result of its impressive collective research will surely be the standard account of the history of Aberdeen for decades to come.

I grew up in the Aberdeen of the 1950s and '60s. My impression of the town was that it was a pretty prosperous place and that elsewhere folk lived in much worse conditions, impressions confirmed by occasional visits to Dundee and Glasgow. The memory of the *blackness* of the latter city when I first visited in 1959 to see the Dons lose 3–1 to St Mirren in the Scottish Cup Final will never leave me. In fact Aberdeen was then one of the poorest cities or large towns in Scotland – even the UK – and with the largest percentage exodus (nearly 10 per cent of the population, 15,000 people, from 1950–70) from any major city. Coupled with a lack of immigration this meant the population was falling at that period. It was also, according to the census of 1951, the town in Scotland with the least number of skilled workers and the highest amount in social class four (semi-skilled) and five (unskilled), and as a result of this and other factors wages were lower than elsewhere.

What I saw as prosperity was in some measure a parsimony and respectability amongst the population, especially the working class, which kept up appearances far better than in other Scottish urban areas where workers with more money, but a different ethos and cultural patterns, were more liable to sink into poverty-generating forms of behaviour. Poverty in Aberdeen was self-managed to a degree almost unknown elsewhere: the city had the largest number of members of the Co-operative Society (50 per cent of adults) anywhere in Scotland and the largest proportion with small savings bank deposits (35 per cent). In this context the renowned Aberdeen thrift comes to be seen as a poverty management strategy. Allied to this, the Aberdonian poor were less likely to call on public and private sources of social welfare than those in other towns.

Oil (the first was landed about a year or so after I left Aberdeen in 1973) has changed our perception of the city so much that it is worth reminding ourselves that the place was never previously a boom town like Glasgow, Paisley or Dundee. Although the city had a large and varied industrial base, apart from the textile industry, organised in huge mills, which looked to make Aberdeen the Bradford of the North until its collapse in 1848–50, Aberdonian industry was small- to medium-scale. The biggest works like the shipyard and the paper and surviving textile mills employed around 1,000–2,000 workers, with most factories having far fewer. The two biggest granite works each employed 100 men and in 1950 two-thirds of trawling companies owned only one boat.[2] Lower concentrations of workers meant lower levels of unionisation (in the 1920s almost 40 per cent of Dundee workers were unionised, compared with just over a quarter in Aberdeen) – and generally lower wages. And the post-1945 mass production industries (NCR (National Cash Registers) employed 6,500, Timex etc) which transformed the economy of Dundee and other Scottish towns never came to Aberdeen, as the city was too far from the markets. The lack of such light consumer industries also limited female (especially married female) participation in the labour force to the lowest of any major Scottish town or city. Living on the Kincorth council estate in the 1960s, I knew no-one in the streets around whose mother worked, apart from the one single mother. I now know why. Partly it was 'respectability' – and partly it was simple lack of opportunity.

Today in Aberdeen, oil boom wages are higher and unemployment lower than the Scottish average; but for those outside the inflated oil industry, higher prices across the board combine with wages still lower than the national average in the non-oil sector. This produces a situation where Aberdeen is possibly the most wealth-polarised city in the country. Respectability and parsimony had previously kept Aberdeen's underclass small, but this is no longer the case. The city does not suffer from urban deprivation and social breakdown on the scale of some areas in Glasgow, but Aberdeen's poor are no longer as good at keeping up appearances as they were, nor is the poverty so confined to specific smallish enclaves as formerly. Because of this, family breakdown, drug and alcohol addiction and crime have spread from former ghettoes to working class areas I remember as eminently respectable (I deal with a couple of these in later chapters). For example, illegitimacy was always much higher in the North East than elsewhere in Scotland (both my grandfathers were illegitimate). Social pressures had reduced this to about 5 per cent in the 1950s; by 1993 34 per cent of all births in the city were to unmarried mothers.

This economic situation, with the city being dominated by small- to medium- scale industry after the 1950s, affected the bourgeoisie as well. The Aberdonian capitalist was poor relative to those elsewhere. From 1876–1913, of the 370 greatest fortunes in Scotland only three were from Aberdeen, compared with 16 from comparable-sized Dundee and 13 from Paisley, the latter town with half the population of Aberdeen. (The three Aberdonians were Duncan Vernon Pirie, a paper maker, John Crombie, a textile capitalist, and John Fyfe, a granite master.) As a consequence few of the industrial figures accumulated the financial wherewithal to make any great inroads nationally in business. And the expand-or-die logic of capitalism gradually meant that, unable to expand outwards, Aberdeen's industry became absorbed into larger national and multi-national concerns. The take-over of Ogston's soap works by Tennant's of Glasgow is a good example. Local capitalists also tended not to go in for more than parochial politics; they were essentially local heroes. Pirie, for example, the owner of Stoneywood paper mill, became MP for Aberdeen North, but made no impact on national politics. The local bourgeoisie went to the Grammar School or (increasingly in the 20th century) Robert Gordon's College, then to Aberdeen University, before taking up work in the family firm and living a life circumscribed by the city's physical and mental boundaries.

People who made a national impact from an Aberdeen base tended to be outsiders: Boyd Orr or Dugald Baird in science, James Bryce and Wedgwood Benn in politics. Locals who achieved a wider impact did so by leaving the city, such as Thomas Glover, a key player in Japan's industrialisation, and Alexander Stephen, who became one of the Clyde's great shipbuilders, his Linthouse yard producing ten times the annual output of the entire Aberdeen shipbuilding industry. The elite of Aberdeen appear to have been quite content to be 'big *puddocks* in a wee puddle'. Since the discovery of oil, Aberdeen has produced a couple of entrepreneurs who, unlike their predecessors, can take their place amongst captains of industry of national and international importance. But Ian Wood, directly involved in the oil industry, and Stuart Milne, whose millions were made off the resulting housing boom are exceptions; almost all of the oil industry is foreign-owned.

The relative poverty of the local bourgeoisie affected life in the city. Although there are obvious exceptions, such as the donation of the Duthie Park to the city in 1883 by Elizabeth Duthie of Ruthrieston, the relict of a local boat-building dynasty, there was limited civic philanthropy. Compare not just Glasgow, but Paisley with its Coats' and Clarks' massive charitable endowments. Although local capitalists might get a society painter to do themselves or the wife in oils, there was little widespread patronage of the arts either. As well as producing no political figures of distinction, after the later 19th century Aberdeen produced no architect of note in the 20th century (those who cite Scott Sutherland prove the point)[3], no painters (James McBey the etcher talks in his *Early Life* of the philistinism of Aberdeen and of having to leave the city to get work), and no writers of other than local distinction. Geography made the city a provincial one; its economic development reinforced this isolation, rather than overcoming it. There was thus an element of philistinism about life in Aberdeen, reflected in the fact it was the last Scottish city to have an art gallery (in the 1880s). But there were notable and laudable exceptions. The core of the initial gallery's collection was donated by local granite capitalist Alexander MacDonald, and because of his policy of leaving a legacy restricted to the purchase of works less than 25 years old, the gallery acquired an enviable modern collection. From this basis the gallery has today become possibly the best in the UK outside of the major cities. But MacDonald was an exceptional case in Aberdeen.

Aberdeen had an active musical society round about 1800, but music-making in the city declined afterwards. In an attempt to have somewhere that leading performers could come to, the Music Hall was opened in 1859, but it specialised more in minstrelsy, pantomime and other light entertainments than classical music. Her Majesty's Theatre opened in the 1870s (and later became the Tivoli), but was an early music hall rather than a performing drama location, and even the later His Majesty's Theatre specialised in much the same kind of middle-brow variety repertoire. Aberdeen never developed a repertory company, unlike Dundee or even Perth. The most popular play in Aberdeen throughout the 19th century was the penny-dreadful melodrama, *Rob Roy*.

Keeping the Music Hall and His Majesty's going has been a constant battle in the 20th and 21st centuries. A city which produced the artist Jamieson (the Scottish Van Dyck) in the 17th century, James Gibb, the architect of St Martin's in the Fields in London and Thomas Reid, the great Enlightenment philosopher, in the 18th, and the great architects Archibald Simpson, John Smith and the painters William Dyce and James Giles in the mid-19th century has not added a great deal to this tally since 1850. No-one in the 20th century could accuse what remained of the local Aberdeen bourgeoisie of being high brow in their cultural tastes. When the bibliophile builder John Morgan died in 1907, a curious fact was brought to the attention of his fellow citizens, that, 'Not only did he possess books, he also read them.'

I now understand my disappointment when, as a foundling (or as they were called by then, a foundation boy), I went to Robert Gordon's College in 1960, at which time it was the only boy's fee-paying school in the city and the place where the local elite was educated. I had foreseen myself mingling with intellectuals, expecting them to 'come and go, talking about Michelangelo'. Instead, if they had cultural standards at all, these were – I was to discover – those of their parents, the Scouts' Gang Show and maybe Gilbert and Sullivan; that was about it. The only intellectuals in the place were some of the half-dozen bursary boys, reading their Jean-Paul Sartre and Camus and trying to

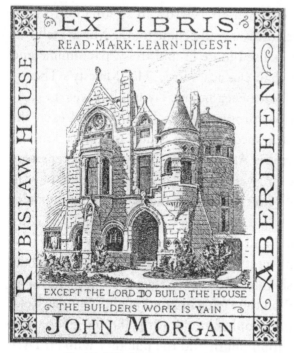

God Builds the Bourgeois House
The book mark of John Morgan, master builder and bibliophile, shows his fine house in Rubislaw. Note that there is a misprint on the *Ex Libris,* which has been hand-corrected. Was Morgan too mean to have another (corrected) set printed?

see Torry as the *Rive Gauche.*

But there was local culture, though of a unique kind. Here we draw upon the specific situation of Aberdeen as an industrial city. It is well off the Central Belt and surrounded by a large rural agricultural area, which is equivalent in population to the town itself and which (with the North East fishing villages) was, until the advent of the oil industry, the source of well over 80 per cent of the population of the city. Aberdeen's surrounding countryside was also until relatively recently the source of many of its industrial raw materials such as flax, wool, water and granite. This has led to the possibly unique situation of a large industrial town being dominated by a diluted version of the rural culture which prevailed in its hinterland. Dundee, for example, does not share this relationship with its hinterland.

That rural North East culture, with its unique language and folk ballad tradition, is, with the exception of that of the Celtic Fringe, the richest of any rural culture in Scotland. Its diluted form is the Harry Gordon, Laird of Inversnecky, Cornkister, Bothy Nichts culture that first appeared in 19th century music halls and is still vibrantly alive in the form of shows like *Scotland the What?* It is clear from the relevant sections in *Aberdeen 1800–2000* that the middle classes bought into this culture as enthusiastically as the working class. The recent appearance of the novel by John Aberdein, *Amande's Bed*, which describes working class life in Aberdeen in the 1950s without any of this *schmaltz* is a welcome development, but is conspicuous by its uniqueness. It is an example that needs following.

Geography put Aberdeen where it is, the only large centre of population far from the heartland of Scotland's political and economic life. The great events of history passed it by or left it lukewarm: the Reformation, the Covenanters, the Jacobites and Hanoverians... even devolution, for the city was one of the few places to vote No in the 1979 referendum. It is also lukewarm in religion, with the lowest kirk attendance of any Scottish city. Sectarianism and racism have never been a part of Aberdeen life, one reason being that Catholics formed a tiny percentage of the city's population, less than two per cent in the 19th century, and more exotic immigrants like Jews and non-whites were virtually non-existent till the later 20th century. The secularism of Aberdeen life is bred not of an intellectually enlightened standpoint, but of indifference.

Local issues dominate life. With its claim to be Britain's oldest newspaper, the present-day *Press and Journal* reflects the character of the town well. It sells at almost saturation level and has been described as a weekly local paper which comes out every day.[4] There are well-known stories of the *P&J* announcing that an Aberdeen man had drowned at sea when the *Titanic* sunk, and that a giant turnip had been found at Turriff on the day after the outbreak of World War One. Even if apocryphal, such stories are significant, for they reveal how the town is seen by outsiders. I can proudly claim to have helped to make a modest contribution to the continuation of this tradition. A few years ago one of my books was shortlisted for an award as one of the ten books which 'said most about Scotland today' and I was interviewed by the *P&J*. The article announced 'Torry *Loon* in Line for Literary Prize', and, apart from giving the name of the book, the piece spoke only of where I had been born, lived, gone to school, my parents, sister etc. They knew their audience: these readers were not interested in a daft book, but wanted to know whether they knew the *loon*/knew his sister or most importantly *kent his faither*. The book didn't win the prize, by the way. *Serves him richt.*

The local upper and middle classes have always been fairly luke-warm in their political associations. A moderate Liberalism dominated them (and the city) till World War One, and after that a moderate Conservatism took over. Now, a little slower than elsewhere, this Conservatism appears to be dying and Liberalism returning. Aberdonians were never ones to rush into things. Elements of the working class, however, have at times escaped this *cauldrife* miasma and produced movements and figures which have attained a wider significance. Despite the small scale and scattered nature of industry in the city in the last two centuries, the Aberdonian working class has a surprisingly radical element to its story, from the time of the agitation associated with the French Revolution through to the Chartist epoch and till the foundation of the modern labour movement. Though it never achieved a local cultural hegemony or even, apart from for very brief periods, dominated the political and social agenda of the city, the Aberdonian working class has made notable efforts to connect with the wider world and international socialism.

In the 1890s – way before Glasgow and most other Scottish towns – Aberdeen had a sizeable contingent of ILP (Independent Labour Party) members on the local town council, able to influence legislation in favour of the working class, such as the construction of the city's first council housing. In the same decade, Tom Mann, of the radical Marxist Socialist Democratic Federation (SDF) came within 500 votes of winning Aberdeen North at a by-election, which would have made him the first explicitly socialist MP in Britain.

Under its effective leader Thomas Kennedy, the SDF opposed the Boer War, establishing a long tradition of anti-militarism in the city.

This was followed by Aberdeen witnessing almost the only activities carried out in Scotland against World War One anywhere outside Glasgow. During the by-election campaign in 1917 in Aberdeen South, when, after an anti-war meeting addressed by Ramsay MacDonald had been broken up by drunken soldiers, at the next public meeting the stewards gave some of the potential disrupters a good hiding before the meeting, which ensured their silence during it.

Aberdeen responded in a dramatic, albeit brief, way to the Russian Revolution. The local Trades Council supported the 'Hands Off Russia' campaign and sympathy for Soviet Russia was marked in the May Day demonstration of 1920 in the city. An Aberdeen Communist group was formed by Elgin-born William Leslie, who attended the Third Congress of the Communist International in Moscow in 1921, where he argued that 'Aberdeen was more Red than Glasgow'. And an Independent Socialist and self-proclaimed Bolshevik, A Fraser MacIntosh, was elected as a town councillor for Torry in 1919. Aberdeen North was won by the Labour Party in 1918 – only one of a handful of Scottish seats won and in the town as a whole in the 1920s Labour had around 50 per cent of the parliamentary vote.

The Communist party did very well in Aberdeen North between the wars. On one occasion Helen Crawfurd, an erstwhile leader of the Rent Strike in Glasgow during World War One, gained almost 4,000 votes (the same as an ILP candidate drew a few years later), showing that a solid bedrock of radicalised workers existed in the city at that time. And Aberdonian workers later made an important contribution to the fight against Fascism in the International Brigades in the Spanish Civil War. They also made notable contributions towards the struggle of unemployed workers in the 1930s, leading into London some of the great Hunger Marches, an honour due to them as the contingent which had walked furthest. The post-World War Two scene was similarly marked by many important radical campaigns, with the local Trades Council being active against apartheid and nuclear weapons, and there were considerable strike movements in the 1960s and 1970s which

Election Fever in the 1920s
The local *Evening Express* comments on a by-election in 1928 in Aberdeen North. This was one of the first seats to go Labour in Scotland in 1918, and remained so apart from in 1931. Between the wars the Communist Party put up a good showing here.

carried over into the new oil industry, when workers struggled to organise and fight for their basic rights. And in the radical later 1960s Aberdeen had a libertarian youth movement, stimulated initially by opposition to the war in Vietnam, which was large in proportion to the size of the city, and whose activities had the worried *Press and Journal* devoting a large article to it, entitled simply 'Anarchists!'

It would never do to claim that the Aberdeen proletarian was ever an internationalist to his bones. There remained a certain couthy rapport between Aberdeen workers and their employers, illustrated by the familiar names given by many of the workers to their workplaces; Soapy Ogstons, Stinky Millers etc. To some extent this was a way of cutting the employers down to size. But in another way it indicated that the gulf between classes was not as wide as it was, for example, on Clydeside, where such familiarisation was non-existent. In the 1950s a famous local trade unionist could begin his meetings with the phrase, '*Chiels, fella-cairters and aa loons fa takk tae dae wi the bylermakkers union*'. Unless this can be regarded as a pre-post-modernist self-referential irony, it betokens that a certain parochialism existed amongst the Aberdeen working class as well.

This wee bookie (Aberdonians diminutise everything; it is possibly the only place in the world where the triple diminutive exists, eg, *little wee mannie*) looks at the history of some of the important industrial areas of Aberdeen through an examination of their industries and built environments, and encourages readers to go and walk these areas, seeing their delights for themselves. It also attempts to rescue from relative obscurity not only people from the political world, but also – reflecting wider cultural concerns and my own personal interests – from the climbing world. If Aberdonians are looking for heroes who were more than local, there are one or two candidates here.

I was initially a little resistant to the suggestion of my publisher to work on this book. I knew that, Aberdeen being a smaller place, urban walkabouts could not provide a whole book of material as did my account of Glasgow in *This City Now*. But I had written other articles on the city and with some re-working, and the addition of a couple more new chapters, I realised that they might complement the urban essays and produce a volume. It has been an interesting personal odyssey for me to write it, though I am aware that it is marked by the unavoidable drawbacks, as well as hopefully the advantages of insight, of the perspective of an exile. I have scant hope that it will be well received in my native toun. Rather the response will probably be, '*Fit dis he ken aboot it? He wint awa did he nae?*' I told my publisher this, but fired by tales of local history books in Aberdeen 'walking off the shelves', he wouldn't listen. Or maybe he didn't understand me when I said, '*Aye, bit mebbi nae this ane. They'll mebbi nae like this ane.*'

Despite initially struggling to find my way with this book, it has taken on a life of its own and has moved me from an initially detached and possibly over-critical attitude, towards a positive re-engagement with my native town, and indeed with my own earlier life. *So buggery I care, gin ye like it or no.*

Notes

1   Examples of this exist even in scholarly writing, such as the excellent *Aberdeen in the 19th Century* (1988) ed. JS Smith and David Stevenson. As one example, on p34 we are told that on 'every social statistic available' Dundee was worse than Aberdeen in the early 20th century. True, but Dundee was the worst in the country. The writer does not point out that, Dundee aside, Aberdeen had a higher infant mortality rate (144/1,000 births) than anywhere else in Scotland, higher even than Glasgow. Despite overcrowding being greater in Glasgow, Aberdeen's poor sewage and sanitation levels more than equaled things out. *Waur nor Glesca? Nivver! Leave that bittie oot!*

2   On the trawling industry there is some confusion, as elsewhere on p90 of *Aberdeen 1800–2000* we are informed that in 1912 over 60 per cent of boats were owned by 10 companies with more than five boats each. Either one set of statistics is wrong, or there was a major disaggregation of the industry between 1912 and 1950, which appears surprising.

3   After the classical greatness of Smith and Simpson, the Caledonian Revival of the later 19th century produced some splendid buildings as well. But, as William Brogden said, in *Aberdeen in the 19th Century* (p86), 'The 20th century is another, sadder story.' Actually there are some very good Art Deco buildings from the inter-war period, but in the last half century, especially the last 30 years, there has been nothing bar a few good restorations of older buildings.

4   When Grampian Television started broadcasting in 1961, it announced that its aim was, 'To bring the area to the outside world, and to bring the outside world to the area.' This suggests that there had been a level of previous *dis*connection. The establishment of a Grampian Television is another example of the intense regionalism in what I have elsewhere described as Scotland's Catalonia. The Northern Co-operative Society... the Cairngorm Club...

PLACES

CHAPTER ONE

Hairbouring Regrets?

HAVING WATCHED THE RIVER CLYDE die as a maritime channel over the last four decades, I find it is always uplifting to come to Aberdeen and see the harbour bustling with activity and busy with boats. When I lived in Torry I had a wee doggie, and one of my (and his) favourite walks was around the basins of the harbour, and then back *owir the watter* along Market Street. Watching the folk working in the fish houses, the lorries coming and going, and the boats moving on the face of the water offered delights to the eye – and even to the nose, if the tenterers were firing the kilns and hanging up the herrings to be kippered.

As a kid I was lucky enough to have also, been able to board some of the boats with my father. At that time he worked as a maritime radio engineer repairing the radio and sounding equipment on the trawlers when they were in port. It was exciting for a boy to go on board and sit absorbing smells and sights. A bit later, when my grandfather was a night watchman (a *watchie*) on the trawlers, I would sometimes visit him after being on an under-age visit to some harbour bar, to sober up a little before going home. And a little later again, after youthful night parties, my steps would occasionally lead to the Fish Market, where workmen's early-morning cafés provided a fortifying detox of strong tea and buttered *rowies*. In reality, I probably performed each of these pilgrimages a couple of times, but memory plays tricks and creates traditions out of occasional events. These experiences left me, I suppose, with a romantic, nostalgic view of the area around the harbour. My one regret in exile was that I had never sailed out of it.

I finally achieved that long-held ambition in 1998, on a trip to Shetland, verifying to my delight the old adage that '*Clachnaben and Bennachie/Are twa landmarks fae the sea*' as I headed up the Buchan

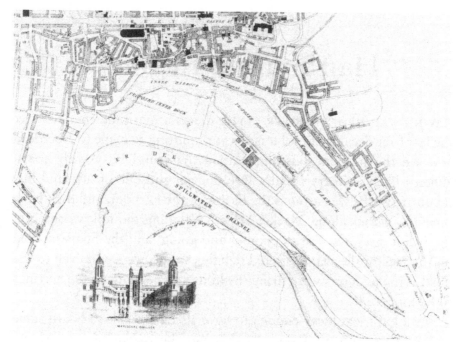

The Changing Harbour and Docks

These two images show the massive changes which overtook the docks and harbour areas after the engineering works of the 1860s, '70s and '80s. Kellas' father was Secretary to the Mercantile Marine Board at this time (see chapter 10).

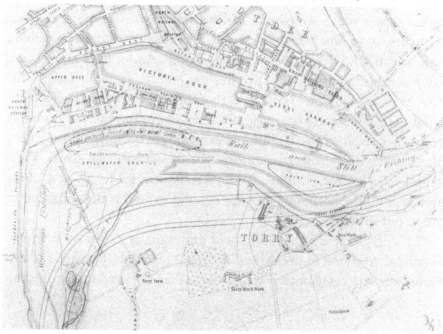

coast. Formerly, as you can see from old atlases, you could sail all down the east coast to London from Aberdeen, and beyond Shetland to Iceland. You could also sail to many European ports, especially those around the Baltic. This meant that in 1917 and afterwards many exiled revolutionaries, such as the aged anarchist thinker Kropotkin, who were returning to Russia, departed from Aberdeen, and representatives of the new Bolshevik government on occasion used the city as their entry point to Britain.

There is a pleasant granite building, now offices, on the corner of North Esplanade West and Market Street. This was originally built more than a century ago as the Torry Tram Depot, and is a good place to start a walkabout, looking across to Torry. Arnold Stavrum was a Norwegian who played for Aberdeen in the 1990s, before being transferred to a team in Istanbul. He was asked what differences this had brought to his life and replied, 'When you look over the Bosphorous you see the spires of the Topkapi Palace, when you look over the Dee you see the fish houses of Torry.' What Stavrum possibly didn't know was that the Dee at this point had been re-engineered between 1871 and '73 into an entirely new channel from its original outflow northwards, and that all the land hereabouts was originally the tidal estuary of the river and not dry land covered in buildings. I didn't know that either when I lived in Aberdeen, and even further changes have taken place in the harbour area since that date.

The first thing my wee mutt would notice now (he was an obser-vant creature) is that, though the odd fish house remains along North Esplanade East, most of the territory here has been given over to the various support facilities of the new oil industry. In addition, much of the area around Mearns Quay and Albert Quay has been blocked off and posted with warning signs threatening prosecution under some of the anti-terrorist legislation brought in recently. Other parts of this area are being demolished for redevelopment, so I hastened along Albert Quay to the new Fish Market on Albert Basin. All this was also originally tidal land, till the 1880s when the Albert Basin and the surrounding quays were formed.

The old Fish Market was no marvel of architecture, but it had a certain demotic charm and was open to the quay which made its goings-on visible. The new one is a tin shed which fronts the waters where a few fishing boats were berthed. The Albert Basin was where most of the trawling fleet used to berth and be serviced. In 1969 it was the scene of much activity during the trawlermen's strike, when most of the 150 trawler fleet were laid up in the basin. During the strike the self-employed inshore fishermen attempted to land their catches at the Fish Market to take advantage of the strike, but were prevented by mass picketing and re-directed their boats to Fraserburgh and Peterhead.

One group which used to work here were the 'lumpers', or fish market porters, whose job it was to unload the fish from the boats and set it out for sale. This was a clannish group, strictly father to son, and the most closed of closed shops. No one dared touch a fish except for the highly organised and highly paid lumpers. One member of the Championship-winning Aberdeen football team of 1955, when the players were refused a wage rise for their success, went back to his job

Fish Market, around 1900
A busy scene, familiar to many until the 1970s, and the collapse of the trawling industry in that decade. Most of the berthage for the fishing fleet was soon to be occupied by oil industry vessels.

as a fish market porter as it was better paid than football. The lumpers were a separate group from the dockers who handled cargo in the port, and a great bone of contention was always the demarcation of frozen fish. Was it cargo (dockers' work) or fish (lumpers' work)? An important question if your livelihood depended on it. Often these workers appeared to be more often at each other's throats than in dispute with their employers. One unusual lumper was Alex Harwood. Firstly, he was English and secondly, he painted almost every trawler working from Aberdeen in the inter-war period. Executed in a flat, naïve but pleasing style, many of his works can be seen in the Maritime Museum (an example of his work can be seen in the colour picture section).

Like the other harbour areas, most of the Albert Basin now appears to be given over to oil industry vessels. You could formerly walk all around the Albert Basin, along Commercial Quay and then back along Blaikie's Quay on the Victoria Dock. (After early harbour improvements by such as Smeaton and Telford, this was Aberdeen's first modern dock, completed in 1848.) Most of the eastern part of this land is now restricted-access oil company territory and Black's Lane is about as far as you can get. The Aberdeen Harbour Board seems determined to separate the population from its maritime heritage as much as it possibly can. Towering over the Victoria Dock is the concrete monstrosity of the Salvesen Tower. It cannot be argued that there is much built environment here that goes beyond functional plainness at best. Despite this disappointment, the excitement, the colour and the movement of the oil support vessels in the Victoria Dock is palpable and exciting.

The oil industry transformed Aberdeen, bringing both immigrants to the town and prosperity for many inhabitants. Initially there was the Wild West atmosphere of a frontier industry. Safety was summed up in the reported comment of one oil boss, 'Fall off that derrick, bud, and you are fired before you hit the deck.' The employers – many American and anti-trade union – used blacklists and the technique of sub-contracting to prevent workers' organisation in the industry. Ironically the oil employers have recently officially abolished the blacklist which they claimed for decades did not exist. As wages were high many workers went along with this cowboy capitalism, until such incidents as the Piper Alpha disaster in 1988, where 167 workers died, showed that truly '*Ye cannae spend a dollar when yer died.*' Since then both workplace organisation and safety have improved in the industry, though how these improvements will survive the inevitable decline of oil is open to question.

A further point of interest in the Upper Queen's Dock is the Northsea (formerly P&O) ferry terminal to Orkney and Shetland at Jamieson's Quay, whence I sailed in 1998. Aberdeen has always been the mainland link with Orkney and Shetland, as Glasgow formerly was for the Hebrides. But the relationship was different. Some from the Northern Isles migrated to Aberdeen, but their numbers were nothing like those of the Highlanders that moved to Glasgow. In the 1960s the main group from these islands living in Aberdeen was university students, who were a famously clannish lot, drinking in the same bar and frequently going home to the islands at weekends. The Northern Isles never influenced Aberdeen the way the Western Isles did Glasgow, alas.

Back at Market Street we come to the site of the former railway goods station, which is at the time of writing being redeveloped as a massive shopping, residential and leisure centre. It is possibly ill to judge during the construction stage, but this looks like it will match almost everything thrown up in Aberdeen over the last four decades in its ghastliness, if the already opened new bus station which forms part of this redevelopment is anything to go by. It is dangerous to make categorical statements, but here is one. There has been scarcely a single building of architectural merit or originality put up in this city for many decades; oil money has disfigured, not transfigured, Aberdeen. And this is not only in the spillage of uglification that stretches miles north and south of the city in warehousing estates, but inside the town itself. The money poured in and the councils (both the then Grampian region and Aberdeen District) had no need to look, as other places had, for heritage and conservation to provide alternative revenue flows, so an anything-goes approach to development was adopted.

The oil companies were over a barrel; there was nowhere for them to go but Aberdeen, which had every card in its hand, and the town could have got a far better deal out of the multinationals than it did in the boom years. Shetland certainly did.

A little diversion along Guild Street past the bus station brings us to further redevelopments going on around the Joint Station, which opened during World War One. This was Scotland's last major station to be built and is a small masterpiece by the architect JA Parker. The new development will, incredibly, block the frontage of the Joint Station from view. In the 1960s Glasgow blocked the view of Queen Street Station from George Square with a hotel extension – but this is almost 50 years later than that, and such atrocities should have stopped. Opposite the Joint Station lies the famous Tivoli Theatre (formerly Her Majesty's) with its charming Romanesque frontage. This was the town's original music hall from the 1870s, but has been lying in increasing disrepair for decades now, though recently there have been some positive noises about a possible restoration. How on earth can Aberdeen find no money for the restoration of its historic buildings while limitless funds are devoted to inserting glass and concrete monstrosities in all parts of the town?

Retracing our steps back along Guild Street to Trinity Quay, we come to the Shiprow, where amidst a guddle of dereliction and redevelopment, stands the Aberdeen Maritime Museum in a converted church with a new-build glass frontage that allows the visitor constant and delightful views across the busy harbour. This is an excellent, well laid-out and informed museum which narrates the links of the town and the sea from medieval times to the oil age. It also has a neat wee café, but I had spied another watering place...

Most of Market Street south of the former railway goods station was reclaimed from the tidal river course and from the 1890s onwards some fine tenements were built along its west side, with banks and shipping offices on the ground-floor level and housing above. The buildings, such as the Grimsby Chambers with its weather vane spearing a fish and granite balustrade balcony, are all still there, but many are in an unenviable state, making it difficult to guess if they are occupied or abandoned. This is Aberdeen's window on the world, what people see when they arrive in boats, and it could be a waterfront as impressive as many others. I was pondering these things in the Harbour Café, but they didn't seem so distressing as I piled into a plate of stovies with skirlie, the latter a real Aberdonian delicacy of onions and oatmeal, lightly fried in suet. This, I thought, is fare for a fisherman, or a roustabout – or an urban explorer.

The next stage of my walkabout had all originally been part sandy inches, part tidal estuary. I was walking on water. Palmerston Road used to lead to an area which vied with Torry as a fish processing location and I was pleased to see that more of this trade survived than I had expected, though most of the old railway arches are now con- verted to other usages (their coldness originally provided natural refrig- eration for fish processing). The street was named after the great Liberal politician of the 19th century who was popular with the local middle classes, as well as with the skilled workers and their trade unions of the time, which were generally Liberal as well. There were large demonstrations in Aberdeen, as elsewhere, in the 1880s in favour of Gladstone, Palmerston's successor as Liberal leader, and his exten- sion of the franchise to a wider section of the working class, and his struggle over this with the House of Lords.

But Poynernook Road? When a *loon* I was not philistine enough *not* to know that '*poyner*' was the old term (from Low German, like *loon*) for a harbour porter, or dockworker. I had imagined, as you do when young, that the road had always been there, always with the same name. But as it was only laid out in the 1880s, someone had the historical *nous* to give it the appellation, linking it with the past (though it should really have been Poynerneuk, but we'll let that go by). Walking back along Poynernook Road lets you avoid the near- motorway that North Esplanade West has become since the con- struction of the Queen Elizabeth Bridge made it the main southern thoroughfare out of the town, and brings you back to the former Torry Tram Depot. When other places shut down their tram services, they might, for example, convert the former workshops to a museum and put some of the trams there, or donate the redundant vehicles to transport museums elsewhere. When Aberdeen closed its system in the late 1950s, it lined up the remaining vehicles – things of exquisite beauty – near the beach and set them on fire.

The fish have largely gone. The oil will not last forever. Aberdeen's population (despite a recent big extension of the city's area) has actually been declining again for over a decade and as I write this the city council is in the throes of a massive financial crisis, imposing cuts across the board on education, social care and other services. What will happen to this harbour when the wells run dry? Will it die like the Clyde, or will the canny Aberdonians find another niche commodity on which to base local maritime prosperity? Could things go the way of the docks of Dundee and Leith, with the harbour developing into heritage culture and quality housing? If the latter is the way ahead, Aberdeen should take greater care of its built heritage than it has done so far, in the harbour area and elsewhere. Otherwise the managers of its future will only harbour regrets.

I headed over to Torry to buy some rowies, mealy puddings and kippers to take back down south. The idea then struck me: Aberdeen as a future gastro-hub? Na, possibly nae... But they'll need something. They'll need something. The plan recently accepted by the City Council to cover over the unique if underutilised Union Terrace Gardens with a commercially-inspired development, hardly seems to fit the bill as a measure of long term planning and regeneration, though it does fit the tradition established in Aberdeen since oil of taking the quick buck.

CHAPTER TWO

Owir the Watter

'*TORRY'S NAE FIT IT EESED TAE BE,*' I was informed by my friends in the Granite City when I told them of my plans to revisit the place as the basis for an exercise in urban re-discovery, '*It's gey altert noo.*' I left Aberdeen for Glasgow when I was 25 years old, having spent more than half my first quarter century as a Torry *loon*. At that time Torry remained, as it had been for three quarters of a century, the locus of the city's fishing industry. This has subsequently all but vanished and I was keen to find how time had dealt with the place since that economic decline.

The No. 12 bus took me *owir the watter* from central Aberdeen. The term *owir the watter* came to be applied to Torry because the district lies on the far, southern side of the River Dee from Aberdeen, and this gives it a sense of separation from the city proper. Torry was in fact in Kincardineshire till 1891 when it was incorporated into Aberdeen. There was not even a proper bridge to Torry until 1881 when the Victoria Bridge was constructed at a cost of £25,000, after a ferry disaster in 1876 in which 32 people were drowned. Previously there was the Wellington Bridge (Chain Briggie) further up river, but this carried limited traffic and was in an inconvenient location. From the bus I noticed a sign on the bridge proudly emphasising Torry's separateness from the city and stating that it had gained its original charter back in 1495.

I travelled in the bus up Victoria Road, Torry's main artery, till the thoroughfare came to Nigg Bay Golf Club where I got off to start my wanderings, adopting the form of a figure-of-eight circuit that took me three hours and brought me back to my starting point. By that time I had to agree that Torry was *gey altert*, though in many ways it *hidnae changit ava*.

From the golf club there is a wonderful view over Aberdeen

Harbour, still busy and bustling with ships and oil work, though that industry is past its peak in employment terms. When I was a Torry bairn, or even 35 years ago when I left Aberdeen, a different sight would have met the eye in Aberdeen Harbour and the Torry Dock. That would have been the equally bustling fishing industry that made Aberdeen not the oil, but the white fish capital of Britain. Today about a quarter of Aberdeen's employment is directly oil related (with roughly the same amount indirectly so); in the past the same or a greater amount was fishing related. There were about 200 trawlers operating from the port at its height. No one thought it could ever end, but now there are less than a dozen boats working from Aberdeen and the fate of fishing should be a warning about over-reliance on any one industry, including oil.

Walking downhill towards the harbour mouth you still pass the Torry Marine Laboratory, though given the state of the industry you have to wonder how much longer that research facility is viable. I was even more surprised to find Bon Accord Soft Drinks still here, whose lemonades (known in Aberdeen as 'ale') I had consumed large quantities of half a century ago. This firm used to do door-to-door deliveries, so addicted were Aberdonians to 'ale'. The works lies on Sinclair Road, a walk west along which takes you into the built-up area of Torry. The first things you see are the two white cast-iron towers of the Leading Lights, which guided ships into the harbour. This area was known as Auld Torry and it was composed mainly of the houses of the fisher folk from the period before the trawling boom. Their activities were herring fishing and white fish line fishing, both of which went into steep decline, and many subsequently relocated into trawling work. Most of the houses in Auld Torry were demolished in the 1970s, ostensibly because they were substandard, but it is difficult not to believe that the real agenda was to create room for berthage and other facilities for the enormous explosion of the oil industry which took place in that decade. Some fragments of fisher-housing remain off Sinclair Road in Wood Street and Abbey Road, with their former net-drying greens and storage sheds. It is really hard to credit that the rest of the houses were impossible to save.

Torry From the Suspension Bridge c.1900
Looking over to the lums of the fishworks and factories of this burgeoning suburb,
and the tenements recently built to house the workers in the trawling boom.

As I was taking a photograph, I was reminded I was back in
Aberdeen and not in Glasgow, where such an event would have been
a prelude to bravura and street theatre.

'*Fit ee daein? Fa're 'ee?*' inquired a curious Torry wifie, stopping
in mid *claik* with her neighbour.

I explained my photographic purpose. This did not placate the
virago: *Fit for? Far's the picter gyan intill?*

Further along Sinclair Road I was pleased to see that some white
fish processing still survives down alleys in an assortment of tin sheds,
amongst the ubiquitous existence of oil facilities and services. Again in
trying to photograph this survival of the past I ran up against a reluc-
tance I had previously experienced in Muslim Morocco, where the
locals think the camera steals the soul. A Torry fish *quine* had to be
extensively placated and re-assured before she would agree to my
request for a photograph. The request for a smile however, did not
produce one, but only a guarded, *Fit wye? Fit dae ee wint a smile for?*
Clearly she thought a suspicious scowl was enough.

The area around Sinclair Road was the heart of the Torry fishing industry, which dated from the introduction of steam trawling in the 1880s. This was the brainchild of a consortium of local business men headed by William Pyper, and soon he and other boat owners were making large fortunes in the industry. At its height there were about 3,000 trawlermen working, but in addition there were a similar number in boat building, box making and ice manufacturing, and a further 4,000 in the city employed in the processing of the fish. When you add to that the distribution network, the industry directly employed over 12,000 people in Aberdeen. With the added indirect employment it used to be said that the city's prosperity '*aa cam oot o' a cod's airse*'. Collapse was sudden. Even in 1970 the industry was still producing almost 2,500,000cwts of white fish – equal to its 1913 peak. But the quadrupling of oil prices in the early 1970s, and the extension and then even greater subsequent extension of Iceland's fishing area in the Cod War, dealt the industry blows which all but killed it.

John Lewis' boatyard specialised in trawler construction and opened in 1917 on the South Esplanade East off Victoria Road. It has long gone (and so too has the earlier John Duthie yard which lay further east) and its site has become an oil industry storage depot, though Lewis United Junior football team still exists. In the 1930s the Aberdeen Fascists tried to hold a meeting here and the car of their leader, Chambers-Hunter, was overturned with him in it. The Fascists returned the next week on the back of a lorry but were driven off by workers from the Lewis yard pelting them with coal. I remember once seeing an old photograph of Lewis workers; one of them was a black man, astonishing in any shipyard, and doubly so in Aberdeen where black people were almost non-existent.

I noticed that Cordiners' box-makers on Sinclair Road has survived the decline in wooden fish box-making (most of the large-scale fish processors have gone), by converting itself to a general timber yard. I lived in Sinclair Road in the late '60s and early '70s and the melting ice, a thin fish bree, from the fish boxes *sypit doon atween the cassies* (granite setts), so that winter or summer, rain or shine, the street stank of fish effluvia. A blind man would have known he was in Torry by the smell. Fish was so plentiful that workers in the industry got a 'fry' on a Friday, which meant as much free fish as they could carry away. Men coming off the boats would be similarly loaded with fish. Shopkeepers, neighbours, publicans and relatives were the beneficiaries of these fries, so abundant that the recipents themselves had to pass on much of the fish. And it wasn't rubbish; cod, halibut, turbot and other fish now astronomically priced, you ate till you were sick of it. No more.

Trawling and its associated processing was always a hard, hard industry, often passed from father to son and mother to daughter. The working conditions in the Torry fish hooses were abominable by any civilised standard. Processing workers regularly lost fingers, or even hands, in the filleting, and hygiene conditions were conspicuous by their absence, leading to boils, abscesses and infections. A wonderful picture of the industry in the '50s and '60s is given by Stanley Robertson in his two books, *Fish Hooses* (1990, 91), and I would not even try to replicate his achievement in describing the work patter and working conditions in the fish sheds. These are almost unique accounts of manual labour by a manual worker. Like many in the industry, Stanley was of the travelling folk, working seasonally. The industry, except in some of the bigger places belonging to national companies, was generally non-unionised, though Stanley comments (without, sadly, describing such an incident) that:

> There wis a code of honour amongst the fishworkers and if somebody hid a right grievance then he got the sympathy of his comrades. I personally hae seen a whole fish hoose come oot on strike cos somebody got a rotten deal fae a boss.

But however hard the landward side of the industry was, that at sea was immeasurably worse. Suffice to say that mortality rates amongst trawlermen were 10 times those of the next highest industry, coal mining. Conditions were unsanitary and hours of work long, often up to two days at a time with hardly a break:

> If ye were fishin in the winter time you were in a lotta dark-ness, you would shoot the trawl at say four o'clock in the

efterneen. You'd maybe have a cuppa tea before it started. Now y'd pull the trawl at maybe seven o'clock at night. At this time ye'd hae yer supper. Then y'd go forward an start guttin the fish... and it would maybe be half past eleven when ye'd shoot again. Three hoors fae then ye'd pull that trawl again, but durin that space ye was guttin the fish.

So ye went tae yer bed for an hoor and a half... to be called again at half past two or maybe half past three in the morning, t'do the same process, pull the trawl, empty the cod end, throw the trawl over the side again.

Work, Welfare and the Price of Fish,
published by Aberdeen City Council in 1995

Frustration at these primitive conditions culminated in the long, drawn-out, trawlermen's strike of 1969, when the port was closed, and you really could walk across Aberdeen Harbour on the berthed boats. This was one of the city's largest and longest industrial disputes.

It was the white fish steam trawler boom that transformed Torry from the quaint fishing village at Auld Torry into one of Aberdeen's most prosperous and populous suburbs with over 10,000 people by 1914 – more than 10 times the 1881 census figure. These new arrivals were largely accommodated in the granite tenements which went up in a couple of decades, and folk came seeking work not only from Scottish fishing villages around the north-east coast, but also from the east coast of England. My grandfather came to Aberdeen pre-1914 from Lossiemouth, while my grandmother moved up from North Shields; both were from fishing backgrounds. These incomers were soon assimilated into an area that was the closest knit in Aberdeen and had the broadest Doric speech. Often whilst the men worked on the boats, the women worked in the landward industries: fish processing, net making and so on. Intermarriage was also common amongst folk in the industry.

Most of the Torry tenements are still there in Victoria Road, Grampian Road and Menzies Road – the latter street you come to by crossing Victoria Road from Sinclair Road. The housing was solid, but most flats were small. In Sinclair Road the houses were mainly room and kitchen until the 1970s, with outside toilets, an aspect which even then was pretty standard. The fact that the toilets were by then on the landings rather than outside in the back courts, was the only real improvement that had been made since the houses were built about 1900. The flat I occupied once I left home had no hot water system either, other than kettles, and the residents before me had been two adults and three children. Since then both flats on each landing of my old tenement have been knocked into a decent-sized one, with modern facilities like baths and inside toilets.

While the fishing workers once lived in Torry, as I walked around the area I didn't get the impression that they have been replaced by oil industry employees. In fact, going along Menzies Road there is a definite feeling that the benefits of the oil boom have passed Torry by, and by Aberdeen standards, the housing stock is in need of sub-stantial restoration. Many of the shops in Victoria Road have closed down, and those which remain are not of the same quality as formerly. And, more than in most areas of the town, you see here the margin-alised, the visibly ill, the clearly drug addicted. Even during the oil boom's height, house prices and rents in Torry remained low, which is probably why much of Aberdeen's recent Polish immigrant community has settled there. Apparently, their language classes feature the local Doric as well as English.

At the end of Menzies Road is HMP Craiginches, built in 1891, a forbidding-looking building. It has the dubious record of having been the site of the last hanging in Scotland, that of Henry Burnett in 1963. Though don't imagine therefore that Aberdeen was a lynch-mob town; the last execution before that one was in 1857. It is a good position to turn up Grampian Place and start heading down Walker Road. Here there is a hardly less forbidding-looking building than Craiginches. It is not a prison but Walker Road Primary School, where under the door marked BOYS, I began my illustrious education over half a century ago. My first day was a disaster. My mother had told me not to lose my coat, so I refused to take it off in class and was smacked over the hand with a ruler – I was only five! – by a female teacher. My despair was deepened when I got home and told my mother about the injustice, and she clouted my lug '*for nae daeing fit the teacher telt ye*'.

The jannie was sweeping the playground and agreed to let me in to photograph the school. He accepted that Torry had seen better days, insisting that the oil money had all gone elsewhere, and the closed-up shops here and on Menzies Road told the same tale.

Walker Road was the birthplace in 1899 of Scott Sutherland, the famous local architect after whom the local School of Architecture was named, though he moved and attended primary school elsewhere. It has to be admitted however that, fine folk though they are, Torry *loons* and *quines* have not figured prominently amongst the celebrities of the wider world.

Back on Victoria Road it was all bustle, with folk going about their business. I discovered the area had not changed in some ways when I went looking for a refreshment; Torry, it would appear, remains a cappuccino-free zone. The only watering place I could discover was The Torry Teapot, where huge mugs of tea lay atop formica tables, behind which portly Torry wifies sat smoking tabbies, with *heidsquares huddin doon* their curlers. It could have been a scene fom 50 years ago. My coffee request produced a spoonful of Nescafé and some *hait watter* and instead of the croissant I had a pair of Aiberdeen *rowies*, a delicacy besides which the croissant palls. These were originally made with lard, not butter (or now, vegetable oil) and designed to last the length of a trawling trip without going off.

Fortified, I proceeded up Victoria Road, and noticed the Victoria Gospel Hall was still functioning. In fact, walking around Torry the amount of missions and kirks and suchlike still there was a surprise, though remembering the religiosity of fisher folk, perhaps it should not have been. If a tin hut was not one of the last fish hooses, it would turn out to be a gospel hall. As I kid I used to be sent to the Victoria Hall for the good of my soul, and I remember once the lay preacher, one of the local fish merchants, telling us bairns we were all sinners and would burn in Hell. A much better place was the Torry Cinema just down from the Halls, which we used to call The Torryers.

Opened in 1921, it closed its doors in 1966. After becoming one of the city's first supermarkets, it is now the site of new housing. This was our Saturday morning Heaven where for coppers you got Tom Mix, Gabby Hayes, Fatty and Skinny (aka Laurel and Hardy) and others. I would like to claim we gained admission with jam-jars as payment, but that was not the case.

Grampian Road leads off Victoria Road where the Torry Library still stands, and then it was up the brae to Glenbervie Road where I spent another, earlier period of my youth. It's a steep pull up the hill to where tenemented Torry ends and the housing from the inter-war period of the 20th century begins. But just at the last block of tenements on Glenbervie Road I found a couple of relics of the past. Aitken's Bakery, which long produced the finest rowies in the land, still survives here. I remember the smell of these baking and sometimes a rowie was thrown in amongst the broken biscuits when you asked the bakers, '*Ony brokners, mannie?*'

Next door (we are in Torry after all) is still found the Sally Anne, another dumping ground for bairns in pre-TV days, to get them off parents' hands. I used to go to a Youth Club there, which ended with a tambourine banging and singing session, and a plate of beans or peas. I don't know if these Salvation Army visits did my moral fibre much good, as I recall that we had various parodies of the hymns, including one (others, such as the parody of 'What a Friend we have in Jesus', are unprintable) which went, to the tune of 'Deep and Wide', '*Soapy watter, soapy watter, My cup's fulla soapy watter.*'

Further along Glenbervie Road is more evidence of change. What I remember as the former bookies is now a Pakistani grocer's, the nearest Torry gets, I think, to multiculturalism. *Naething bit fite faces hereabouts*, I was thinking. But immediately I realised I had done Torry's internationalist credentials a disservice. How could I think this of my virtual cradle and the place that elected Fraser Mac, an Independent Socialist and self-proclaimed 'Bolshevik', as a councillor in 1919? That had a black worker in Lewis' boatyard, as earlier mentioned? I had also momentarily forgotten that in the later 1960s and early '70s there was, at Walker Place, what we in those politically incorrect days called The Chinky Chipper. This oriental establishment broke the monopoly of Tony's Chipper in Menzies Road, and meant that as a change from to the cheapest thing on Tony's menu (a fritter supper made of ingredients you would not have wanted to know about) you could now get an exotic alternative, a pineapple (from a tin, of course) fritter supper for the same price. Torry somehow never built on this early brush with sophistication and I noticed that the Chinky Chipper is long gone. (So too, is Tony's.) But to get back to Glenbervie Road...

Its four-in-a-block garden suburb houses were very desirable when I lived there with my parents and sister in the 1950s, but now there is an air of malaise, difficult to define, about the place. Dropping down Mansfield Road (The Manser) takes us back to Victoria Road and on the left is an interesting building, the former St Peter's Episcopal Kirk, dating from 1897. Originally built for the influx of English fishermen into Torry, the building is now converted into sheltered housing flats and stands out from the surrounding grey with its rich ruby-red granite, uncommon here. My mother once let the pram I was in hurl down The Manser (an accident, she claims), and had a mannie not stopped it in full flight, I would not be writing this today. '*Mair's the peety*', I can imagine some readers muttering.

The eastern end of Victoria Road is where the best housing in Torry is located, a series of modest middle class granite villas. Further on, behind the Balnagask Day Centre, is the oldest structure in Torry. Enclosed within a stone dyke is what as kids we used to call The Moundie (like everything in Aberdeen, the location is diminutised). This was the site of our furious coxie-coosie games, between pairs, or more, of *loons* sitting on each ither's shulders. One pair would hold the summit and try to prevent the other pair dislodging them, singing, '*I'm the king o' the castle, Get doon ye dirty rascal.*'

Coxie-coosie fights were pushing and shoving matches, coalie-bug (coal-bag) fights were where one person was carried on another's back – not shoulders – and generally these used sticks as weapons. I did not know then that The Moundie was actually Torry Motte, almost 1,000 years old, a fortified earthwork long before our childish battles.

Back at Nigg Golf Club I recalled other games and headed downhill for the Bay o' Nigg.

Many Aberdonians went to the beach, often for the fun of watching the shivering *Glesca keelies* on holiday. But that was far from Torry and anyway we had our own beach at Nigg. Old pictures show families at Nigg Bay having picnics with prams. This was not just because there were a lot of bairns in the 1950s, but also because in pre-car days the pram doubled as a carrier for picnic paraphernalia; toys, food, kettles etc. Memories of driftwood fires and black alecks (soot in the tea) will never leave me; nor will those of the coldness of the waters of the North Sea. I never stayed in long enough to learn how to swim.

On the way down to Nigg Bay lies St Fittick's Kirk, a picturesque ruin looking towards Balnagask. The latter is the overspill pre- and post-1945 housing scheme where the majority of Torry folk now live, but which has little of real interest to show (beyond the splendid Art Deco Tullos Primary School built in the 1930s), though its setting beside Nigg Bay and below *The Grumps* (Gramps), as the broom-covered hills to the south are called, is pleasing. *The Grumps* was another area we played in as kids and I remember collecting blaeberries for my mother to make jam; what child would do that nowadays? It is amazing in retrospect how far we gangs of children, all under 10, ranged from home, with never a note of parental concern. They had no idea where we were, and never asked. *Nae Risk Assessments in yon days.* St Fittick's Kirk has many interesting gravestones, the most significant being those of Aberdonians killed by Montrose's troops in the Battle of Aberdeen in 1644.

Greyhope Road curls round towards Girdleness Lighthouse from Nigg Bay. Originally called Griddleness because its shape resembled that cooking utensil, a slip of the tongue created the present name. This name in turn applies to Robert Stevenson's 1833 lighthouse standing here, surely one of his most aesthetically pleasing constructions, a slender spire overtopping 130ft. Below it is found the foghorn whose haunting calls I remember hearing at night in bed when I was young. You really have to know the original story of the Turra Coo

(Turriff Cow) to understand the pun, and it is claimed that this foghorn was known locally to some as the Torry Coo (though others deny this story as nothing other than an urban myth) from its long-drawn moan. The circuit of Greyhope, which is really a circuit of a huge golf course, twists back to give another fine view of Aberdeen, and the remains of the Torry Battery.

One lives in an unreflective world when young. We played here on the then crumbling but now stabilised battlements as bairns, bird-nested in the masonry cracks (now forbidden) and generally risked our lives, without even wondering what the structure was. Built against the threat of a feared French invasion in 1860, the battery was manned until World War Two when it actually saw military action, shooting down a German plane. After the war, as with other places in Aberdeen, homeless people squatted within its walls until they were re-housed in 1953. The Battery is a Scheduled Ancient Monument and

Squatters in the Torry Battery
Probably in the 1930s by Leonard Pellman, looking out over the harbour towards Fittie.
Aberdeen saw much similar direct action on homelessness in the mid 20th century,
though little has been written about it.

breeding ground of several rare species of bird including the protected Ortolan Bunting, which I had never heard of. *Fan I wis a loon I didnae ken there wis mony mair birdies nor doos, seagulls and spurdies*, but there you are, Torry is now on the twitchers' itinerary. Back along Greyhope Road brings you to the golf club and a bus back to town, or a walk down Victoria Road's entire length and back to Victoria Bridge. Here a large vacant site on the right beside the river is all that remains of the house and workshop of a family of salmon netters who swept the tidal waters of the Dee daily for all the time I lived there. Like much else, they have gone from Torry. *It's nae fit it eesed tae be. But Torry loons and quines are naething if nae tough, and I'm sure they'll survive owir the watter.*

Note

Aberdeen City Council has produced three Torry Trails recently, viz.
Torry Urban Trail
Torry Coastal Trail
and
Torry Churches Trail.

www.aberdeencity.gov.uk

CHAPTER THREE

Fit Wye tae Fittie?

ASKED OF ANYONE IN ABERDEEN, the question '*Fit wye tae Fittie?*' would probably produce immediate directions, since '*aabiddy kens far Fittie is*'. Indeed the informant will probably claim that his/her '*grunny came fae Fittie*', or even that he or she themselves did. For Fittie is a Shangri-La to many Aberdonians, a place remembered fondly despite the fact that it virtually no longer exists, or maybe because of that fact. For, almost uniquely in Aberdeen, Fittie has suffered the fate endured by so many districts in Glasgow, of being almost completely obliterated by redevelopment. Most of the housing was demolished and the population decanted elsewhere. It is *Fittie nae mair*.

If you are looking for a bus to get you there, it will say FOOTDEE. If you buy a street map of the city, it is the same name you must look for in the index. However, Fittie is not an Aberdonian corruption of Footdee; the reverse is true. Footdee appears to be an anglicised, possibly Victorian, rendering of the correct historical term. Indeed Fittie became world-famous as far back as 1654. In the atlas of the world published in Amsterdam that year by Blaeu, there is a map of Aberdeen and Banff by Robert Gordon of Straloch. Slightly to the west of its current location, roughly where Waterloo Quay is now, lies the settlement of 'Futty'. John Slezer's *Theatrium Scotia* of 1693 shows a view of Aberdeen from south of the River Dee – with the houses of Fittie visible. This illustration also shows the Blockhouse, a small fort designed to protect Aberdeen's harbour.

From these origins Fittie came to extend over much of the Parish of St Clements. In the 19th century industrial developments filled the area between Fittie village and Aberdeen city proper with mills, shipyards, chemical works, timber yards and railway marshalling yards for the docks. Waterloo Station opened in the 1850s and was the original terminus for the Great North of Scotland Railway. It replaced and was built over the route of the former Aberdeen canal which reached Fittie in 1805. Fittie/St Clements became one of the most overcrowded areas of the city, with generally poor housing conditions. It was, and remains, a very neatly defined area. To the east lies the sea wall and the North Sea. To the south originally flowed the Dee till its 19th century re-direction and replacement by the Victoria Dock. The Beach Boulevard defines Fittie to the north and on the west the tracks of the railway to the goods depot for the harbour cuts the area off from the town centre. This compactness, and the wealth of historical and architectural heritage in Fittie, makes it an ideal urban ramble.

Dropping down from the Castlegate and crossing the railway bridge known locally as the 'Tarrie Briggie' at Castle Terrace brings you to Fittie. The first street you come to is Cotton Street on the left. The street was named after the Bannermill Cotton Works established on the Queen's Links behind Fittie in the 1820s. Its owner was Alexander Bannerman, a paternalistic employer for the time and Aberdeen's first MP, from 1832–47, when he stood as a Liberal. Cotton Street consisted largely of poor working class housing dating from the mid-19th century. In the wonderful collection of Aberdeen oral history, *Work, Welfare and the Price of Fish*, Cotton Street in the 1930s was described by one resident:

The Bannermill
One of Aberdeen's early large scale textile factories, owed by the Bannerman family. Alexander Bannerman became Aberdeen's first post Reform MP, from 1832–47. Conditions in this mill were generally better than elsewhere.

Some o' the faimilies were in a state o' sheer desperation, and the conditions they were living in were absolute slums. We were considered weel aff in Cotton Street because we'd a sink inside! That attic folk nivver had a sink inside and there was one toilet, an ootside toilet for six faimilies, the average faimily being five or six.

I remember Cotton Street from the 1960s, when I had a friend who lived there. Families were by then much smaller, but the houses still only had outside toilets in the back green. This had formerly been not uncommon in Aberdeen tenements, but was a rarity by then. Not only that, but some also had outside sinks – with only cold water – on the landing, shared between two flats. Nevertheless these buildings were spotless, the linoleum on the wooden close stairs polished to perfection. These houses are all gone now, demolished in the mid-1970s, and Cotton Street has become a clutter of storehouses, yards and warehouses. The main feature of historical interest is an old meal mill, still standing on the north side of Cotton Street but now put to use as storage space.

Miller Street takes you further into Darkest Fittie, and between Baltic Street and Garvock Wynd on the left lies a rickle of storage facilities and other light industrial users. Till recently this was the sight of the famous, or possibly infamous, Sandiland's Chemical Works, later SAI Chemical Works, which was subsequently taken over by the giant ICI company. Its huge lums used to pour out noxious fumes, which, if the wind happened to be from the west, were blown out to sea. It mainly produced agricultural fertilisers and has had the honour of being featured in a novel about Aberdeen life in the 1950s. Sandlilands appears in John Aberdein's *Amande's Bed*, disguised as Scottish Fertile but instantly recognisable as 'Stinky Miller's' from the odours produced by the bones, guano and other raw materials used. The reek in Fittie was compounded by the presence next door of the Corporation Gas Works, whose waste products provided some of the raw materials for the chemical factory.

St Clement's Street leads on from Miller Street and here lies St

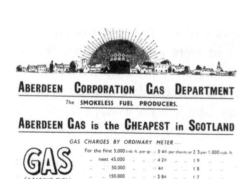

Gas Works Advert
With its reek added to that of the chemical works, the Corporation Gas Works made sea bathing in Aberdeen an especially bracing experience with a unique view. *But fit fine cheap gas!*

Clement's Church, which is well worth a visit. This church was built in 1828 as the area's population was expanding rapidly. It was designed by John Smith, possibly Aberdeen's greatest architect of the early 19th century. The church sadly lost its tower and, with depopulation, its congregation also. It is currently disused, though it may possibly be a future store for the city archives. Its graveyard, however, still contains a fascinating collection of gravestones going back many centuries and recording the maritime history of St Clement's parish. As well as memorials to sea farers, there are monuments to the local shipbuilding families; the Duthies, Halls and Stephens.

One of the Stephens' tombstones is almost a history of Scottish shipbuilding. Alexander Stephen was born in Aberdeen in 1795 and his memorial records that he was a 'Shipbuilder in Aberdeen, Arbroath, Dundee and Glasgow'. He started with clippers in Aberdeen, moved on to whaling boats in Tayside and finally started building steel ships at Linthouse in Glasgow in the 1850s, where his works became one of the three great Govan yards, each employing 5,000 men. But Stephen is buried in Fittie.

The graveyard is a lovely place, but even on a sunny day the wind is snell off the North Sea and should encourage you to keep moving. At the corner of Links Street is one of the few remaining tenements in Fittie, where most of the housing was deemed substandard and beyond renovation. As the area was re-zoned for commercial development, this resulted in a no new-build housing policy in the area, but if you look hard enough you can still find a few inhabited buildings. Just at the end of St Clement's Street, where it meets York Place, is another building by John Smith, which dates from the 1820s. This was built as a combined warehouse and residential development, and as well as hosting what must be one of the last shops in Fittie, the building has evidence of being at least in part still residentially occupied. There are three pubs left in Fittie, since people still work here, but all of the area's many churches have closed (though there is still a mission hall in Auld Fittie), as have its three primary schools and former junior secondary school. It is hard to believe that a community of several thousand people once inhabited these deserted streets.

Just off York Place, on the left, is the depot of the Shore Porters' Society, a warehousing and removals firm which was originally based nearer to the harbour. It moved to Cotton Street in 1877 before relocating its main depot to its present site. This society is unique in at least two ways. Firstly it is the oldest surviving company in the world, dating from the 15th century, and secondly it is still run on semi-cooperative lines, for the benefit of its employees. In fact, it is unique in three ways: the society admitted women members as 'poyners' (porters), provided they could carry 1cwt on their backs from the Blockhouse at Fittie to Broad Street in central Aberdeen. *Nae bother for a Fittie fishwifie.* Whether any actually took up the challenge, I don't know.

The area within the angle formed by York Street and York Place is now occupied by bustle created by the servicing of the oilfields of the North Sea. But how much busier and more bustling it was in the days when this was the location of what was, after 1850 and the collapse of much of the city's large-scale textile manufacture, probably Aberdeen's biggest industrial undertaking: Hall, Russell and Co., Shipbuilders. Aberdeen's shipbuilding could never rival that of the Clyde, but in its heyday in the 1950s and '60s, Hall Russell's was the biggest shipyard in Scotland outside Clydeside, with 1,500 workers. Its key to success was versatility, building a wide range of medium-sized boats, from tankers to cargo boats, fishery vessels and even sailing ships. As with other local shipyards, Hall Russell's suffered from the decline of the trawling industry, most of whose boats had been locally built.

Like shipyards elsewhere, Hall Russell's was strongly unionised, with a well-functioning shop stewards' committee. 'I was convener at Hall Russell's. [The new apprentices] came in on Monday and as convener I addressed them on Tuesday and made it quite plain that they joined the unions. It was always accepted.' (Jim McCartney, in *Work, Welfare and the Price of Fish*). In the post-war period Russell's was probably the most strike-prone works in Aberdeen, though (as with shipyards elsewhere) much of the conflict stemmed from craft militancy and inter-trade rivalry. It was one of the few places in the city where the Communist Party had a significant industrial presence.

Hall Russell's most famous boat was not its biggest; the yard built (originally as the fisheries research vessel *Sir William Hardy*) the ship which was to become the Greenpeace *Rainbow Warrior*, sunk in the South Pacific by French secret agents when Greenpeace was protesting against France's nuclear testing. The most famous boat ever built in Aberdeen was not however built at Hall Russell's, but at the smaller yard of Walter Hood and Co., also in Fittie. This was the *Thermopylae*, one of the fastest-sailing ships ever constructed, which beat the Clyde-built *Cutty Sark* on the China Run, though the latter is often inaccurately stated to have been the swiftest ship powered by sail. After the clipper era with its wooden sailing ships, Aberdeen should really have collapsed as a shipbuilding location,

Hall Russell Advert
For a long time one of the city's main employers, producing a wide variety of smaller craft. Eventually too these niche markets disappeared, and the yard closed.

as it was far from sources of coal and iron, the foundations of the industry after 1870. The local industry was saved by the introduction of steam trawling in the 1880s, and trawlers comprised the bulk of the local yards' outputs thereafter.

Like Sandilands in *Amande's Bed*, Hall Russell featured in fiction as Gowan and Gloags, located in the district of Footforthie in Lewis Grassic Gibbon's novel, *Grey Granite*, published in the Depression year of 1934. Gibbon is regarded by many as Scotland's greatest 20th century novelist and I would not want to dispute that. But in my view the picture drawn of working class life in John Aberdein's novel is superior to that given by Gibbon. Gibbon was of farming stock and a cub reporter in Aberdeen after World War One. He had little experience of working class domestic and industrial life, and it shows in *Grey Granite*. Aberdein on the other hand grew up in a working class area, with people who worked in industrial employment and who – since they were political – talked about that and other aspects of proletarian existence. In addition, Aberdein's use of dialect captures the richness and complexity of the local Doric more accurately. Gibbon made enormous concessions in his use of the language, dropping for example the essential fricative of the North East (*fit, fan, foo*) as well as the absolutely fundamental *ken*, for knowing. Aberdein's rendering of the dialect is flawless, both in vocabulary and timbre, and the only regret is that he limits its use to dialogue and one example of narrative, rather than writing the whole book in Doric.

Gibbon also describes Fittie in his essay 'Aberdeen' in *The Scottish Scene*: 'Footdee sleeps with its silent shipyards and factories, with great rusting cranes lifting their unmoving chains in the air.' Maybe it was short-time working in the '30s that enabled the Hall Russell football team to practice and become the only team from the entire North East ever to win the Scottish Junior Cup, in 1934. The yard recovered with the war, though it was hit by accident in an air raid in 1940 when a German plane jettisoned its bombs and killed 32 people. Its competitive position was probably not increased by the acquisition of the nearby and similarly named yard of AS Hall in the 1950s. Even by the backward standards of British industry, Hall's stood out. One worker remembered:

A Hall and Company was the most antiquated shipyard in Britain. I was workin wi machinery that was originally steam driven. And durin the war a shipyard inspector cam round. The foreman took him round and the inspector said, 'I've seen many antiquated shipyards in Britain but I never saw a yard like this.'

Work, Welfare and the Price of Fish

The combined yard had full order books in the two decades after the war, but with even the Clyde yards struggling from 1970 onwards, its days were numbered. Hall Russell's closed in the early 1990s, though some of the granite rubble-clad buildings remain around York Place and are still used as storage. The clang of the hammer sounds no more from the yard and its Hall Russell's Male Voice Choir is also silent. One worker from the yard was Tammy Lennox. I don't know if he was in the Hall Russell's choir, but he made his contribution to music by fathering the famous singer Annie Lennox. In the Aberdeen Maritime Museum the story of Hall Russell's, as well as that of the other shipyards and the general seafaring history of Fittie, is excellently told. Those interested should also consult the thoroughly researched volume *Footdee and its Shipyards* by Diane Morgan (1993), for a more detailed account than is possible here.

York Street carries you down to the end of the road at Auld Fittie. Despite its name, in relation to Fittie's antiquity it is not that old. Auld Fittie was laid out at the beginning of the 19th century as a planned village for the fisher folk of Fittie. The architect was again John Smith, who left such a mark on Fittie, and the houses were built for rent by the town council, though sold to the occupants in the 1880s. The houses were equipped with tarry sheds for the fishing gear and built in squares round drying greens for the nets. Though the original classical simplicity has been lost due to the addition of upper stories to some houses and extensions to others, the area still has great charm and interest.

This was a close-knit community of inshore fishermen with their own kirk in one of the squares. As late as 1890, 95 per cent of residents

in Auld Fittie were Aberdeen-born, and about the same percentage
were employed in the inshore fishing. The fishermen had a very early
society which functioned both as a welfare organisation and a building
society. I wonder who held the purse strings? For in the 1930s one
observer said the Fittie fisherwomen took their men's money and
gave them only pocket money, adding, 'the women enslave the men
to do their will and keep them enchained under petticoat government'.
Though Auld Fittie remains, its fishing industry, like shipbuilding and
chemicals in 'upper' Fittie, has gone.

Disentangling yourself from the squares of Auld Fittie, you come to
Pocra Quay. This curious name translates as Salmon Net (*pock*) Row
(*raw*). Here there are some delightful buildings, such as the Harbour
Master's Station, or the Roonhoose, set on its magnificent base of
Aberdeen *cassies* (granite setts), and Fittie's war memorial with its
interesting nautical reliefs. Walking back along Pocra Quay gives
engrossing views of Aberdeen's bustling harbour, with ships con-
stantly coming and going, no longer to catch the silver darlings, but
to service the black gold of oil. This route can be continued by passing
along Waterloo Quay (at the western side of the former Hall Russell
yard) and continuing to Church Street which will re-connect you with
Miller Street and then the Castlegate where we started. And Waterloo
Quay is the place, or at least the location of the place, where Fittie
itself started centuries ago. Auld Fittie remains, though not as a fishing
village, but 19th and 20th century industrial Fittie has gone, replaced
mainly by service depots for North Sea oil. But the oil will not last
forever, and possibly in the future we might see Fittie re-colonised
and the area between the city centre and Pocra Quay filling up again
with people. It has happened elsewhere, *foo nae in Fittie*?

CHAPTER FOUR

The Grunnit Hairt of the Granite City

ABERDEEN'S MERCAT CROSS IS undoubtedly 'by far the finest thing of its kind in Scotland', as Lord Cockburn stated in 1841. It stands at the centre of the Castlegate, itself the historical heart of Aberdeen, though the cross was moved the year after Cockburn's comment from its original site somewhat westward. Designed by the master mason John Montgomery in 1686, its arcades are surmounted by 12 panels containing arms of Crown and City, and wonderful portraits of the Stuart monarchs from James I to James VII. Above those rises a Corinthian-topped column, itself surmounted by a gilt marble unicorn.

Ironically for a place later known as the Granite City, this monument was composed in sandstone; it would have been nigh impossible to carve such elaborate features in granite in the late 17th century. Even 200 years later, when the granite industry was at its height, the hardness of the material would have made such a detailed structure very difficult to execute – and to fund. Today the cross stands in a Castlegate that has been gentrified over the past decade or so, pedestrianised with local *cassies* or setts (oblong granite stones), and the surrounding buildings have been given various degrees of a makeover. You can see the idea; pavement cafés, artists' quarter... but this is *Aiberdeen*, a *caul'* place where the wind and *haar* come up from the North Sea and the residents are not of an extrovert, *flaneuring* nature, and at the moment the area has a rather sterilised look. *It's nae Montmartre yet.*

This sterility was not the case when the 'Castler' was the beating heart of the city. Old paintings, such as JW Allen's *The Castlegate* of 1840, show hucksters, beggars and entertainers at the Castlegate, and markets continued to be held there till historically recently, such as the Timmer Market when *loons* and *quines* from the city would get a second Christmas in the form of (originally) wooden toys. Political rallies were mounted, generally by the various left-wing sects trying to lead the masses from the 1880s onwards, and in the 1930s attempts by Mosley's Blackshirts to rally here led to riots. The area was also one where mass meetings of the unemployed were held between the wars of the last century, leading in one case to a police baton charge and several arrests. 'Riotous scenes in the Castlegate' lamented the *Press and Journal* in 1936, later welcoming the stiff jail terms passed out on the riot's 'Bolshevist' leaders. And that's not all.

Before World War Two feeing markets for farm workers took place, as well as recruiting campaigns for the local Gordon Highlanders' regiment, and rallies against sin by the Sally Anne from their Citadel towering over the Castlegate. At evenings and weekends, the court-ship tradition of *wakkin the mat,* which meant parading endlessly up and down Union Street after the cinemas closed their doors looking for a romantic hitch, had one of its termini at the Castler. Most of these activities vanished after 1945, but the Castler still bustled with buses and *fowk* visiting the myriad pubs, many less than respectable, in the area. The makeover may in time recreate this bustle and make the square a sort of Aberdonian Place du Tertre, but from recent visits I feel that this has yet to happen. Some street furniture or statues might help – what about one of Wee Alickie, Aberdeen FC's well-loved cartoon supporter, to match Dundee's marvellous Desperate Dan? Or a series of statues of *sodjers*, feeing *loons*, and of the political agitators and others who have in the past frequented this place? But such imagina-tion is rather alien to the grounded Aberdeen mentality I fear.[1]

An exotic flavour is however given to the Castler by *La Lombarda*, which claims – surely dubiously? – to be Britain's oldest Italian restaurant, dating from 1922. Though Aberdeen had a smattering of immigrants, historically it was the most ethnically homogeneous of Scottish, probably even British, towns, with well over 80 per cent of its population (until very recent times) coming from its North East hinterland. This has tended to reinforce its unique character – as well as its self-contained isolation. Halfway back through time to the foundation date of *La Lombarda*, your writer was trying to impress a young lady by extending her experience beyond the Wimpy Bar and the couple of Chinese restaurants which then constituted the town's international cuisine. (It should be mentioned here that Aberdonian culinary tastes were simple then. Olive oil was not an essential ingredient of cooking or in salad dressings, but something utilised to *louse the cuddis in your lugs afore howkin it oot wi a spunk* (matchstick).) To return to our tale. She (my girlfriend) ordered spaghetti, the only thing on the menu she recognised, but he in his best attempt at Italian pronunciation ordered something more exotic from the wee waitress wifie who looked like a genuine *mamma lombardiana*, only to hear her reply,

There's nae ony taglatelly the day, loon.

The Mercat Cross may be of sandstone, but the buildings on the three built-up sides of the square here are all in solid granite. Though dating from various periods, the composition in an identical stone, which allows for limited adornment, gives the Castlegate a coherent and pleasing visual impact. Many of the buildings were originally the residences of the town's elite or the town houses of notables from the surrounding countryside, as were those dwellings on the 18th century Marischal Street leading from the Castler down to the harbour. This was the city's first planned street, and the first to be laid with *cassies*. But as time passed and the city industrialised and the population soared, these buildings, with their back lands and many vennels and courts leading off them, became overcrowded slums.

On the north side of the Castlegate, a rummage around Albion and Smith's Courts as well as Peacock's Close gives an idea of what these backlands might have been like. Before a series of slum clearances from the later 19th century, they would have stretched much further into Stygian squalour. It was logical that when James Soutar's Salvation Army Citadel was built in the 1890s, in imitation of Balmoral Castle, it was planted in the Castlegate, where opportunities for the devoted band of redeemers were plentiful. Various plans for the redemption of the Salvation Army building itself stalled over the years, though it is now partially renovated as a location for community groups, with a café.

The Castler isn't quite ready for loft apartments and designer living yet, though certainly the demotic 'grot' I remember has gone. The flea market in Justice Street on a Friday where traders sold junk off blankets laid on the ground, Cocky Hunter's store in the former Children's Hospital, a warren of second-hand furniture over several floors, and pubs like the Royal Oak. There in the 1960s, for the price of a pie and peas served on a paper plate (this gained you entry to a 'Supper Dance'), you could drink till the amazing hour of 11pm, amongst the ladies of commercial affection looking for business, they and their potential customers dancing drunkenly amongst the pies, *skyting across the fleer*. Sophisticated, it wasn't.

The pedestrian could spend hours wandering about here, but the writer must move on. Justice Street takes us east to the Beach Boulevard and one of those gigantic roundabouts that make urban pedestrianism occasionally a chore. As you wait for a chance to cross the river of motor traffic here, look up to the right and you will see the former Castle Hill. Here stand two huge blocks of flats built in the 1960s. Aberdeen lost its castle many centuries ago, and before these flats stood the Castlehill Barracks, which were occupied by squatters in the housing shortages after 1945; these folk later had their tenancies regularised. To your left on East North Street lies the step-gabled former Corporation Model Lodging House built in 1899 and in use as such till 1988. The 'Modler', as it was called in that Aberdonian tendency to diminutise everything, lay in the heart of what was generally recognised as the area of Aberdeen's greatest housing needs.

Park Street brings sudden quiet after the din of the Boulevard's traffic, but this was not always so. When younger I remember this area as being overcrowded, with rickles of bairns up every close and a great deal of very poor housing. I had a pal in Constitution Street and coming down here in the 1960s from Kincorth, probably then the most respectable housing estate in the country, I always felt that I was entering bandit territory. New housing and cleared areas have led to the decline in population, and demographic trends added to this have forced the closure of local schools, such as Frederick Street School. In some of the new housing here, in the 1960s, was Willie's Bookshop. This was a place which sold 'men's interest magazines' of the softer porn variety then available. It was also the place where, more in hope than need, we were able to buy our first condoms. But the shop also sold left-wing books and pamphlets and Willie was reputed to be an old ILP-er from the 1930s. Whatever happened to Willie?

Though this was one of the most overcrowded areas of Aberdeen formerly, it had the advantage of easy access to the nearby beach and its esplanade – and before that lay the open spaces of the Aberdeen Links, thankfully never built over. In the 1850s there was a plan to drive a railway through here but the 'Battle of the Links' prevented this and since then the ground has remained sacro-

ABERDEEN

SCOTLAND'S LEADING RESORT

Sun, Sea and Shivering
It was only for a brief period, but in the 1950s Aberdeen was Scotland's leading holiday resort. People froze on a cold beach, whilst behind them the factories of Fittie belched out pollution.

sanct. Carrying on down Park Road you pass the former City Hospital, now flats, and come to the Links at the Broad Hill. Let's climb this little eminence, and have a look around.

The Broad Hill had a moment of historical significance in the 1840s when a reported 20,000 people assembled on its slopes to listen to speeches in favour of the People's Charter, which aimed to give working men the vote. After the speeches, they voted overwhelmingly in an 'unofficial election' to send a Chartist candidate to parliament. In my younger days the Broad Hill had a rather disreputable reputation as a 'courting' spot, associated with the consummation of liaisons formed at the nearby resorts of pleasure on the Beach Esplanade, such as Cadona's amusement park and the Beach Ballroom, the red-roofed 1920s cameo pleasure-dome readily visible from the summit. I imagine that in these more sophisticated times the crannies of the Broad Hill have been replaced by more comfortable (and warmer) trysting spots. One thing that has gone from the Broad Hill is the illegal gambling that flourished up to the 1950s, when large crowds would gather to play pitch and toss, crown and anchor etc. These assemblies were regularly broken up by police raids.

Inversnecky Culture
A programme from the Beach Pavilion from the inter-war years, showing Harry Gordon, whose brand of kailyard humour was immensely popular in Aberdeen at this, and subsequent times.

It is astonishing to think that, 50 years ago, Aberdeen beach with its associated complex of entertainments was Scotland's largest single tourist destination. Even as a boy it would amaze me when I visited the beach baths (I never once even attempted to swim in the sea), that thousands of Glasgow folk would come and sit on that frozen beach, often drenched in *haar*, and sit having picnics beside a sea of perishing coldness. The tourist industry has vanished all but completely and so too has the fishing industry in the North Sea, the mainstay of Aberdeen's economy for almost a century. The vision across the salty waters now shows oil rigs, and the boats servicing them. Hardly a trawler is left. Half a century ago almost 50 per cent of the population was dependent, directly or indirectly, on fishing; today roughly the same number depend on oil. We have seen the replacement of one dangerous economic dependency by another.

Descending on the northern side of the Broad Hill brings you to Pittodrie Park, home of Aberdeen FC, which was founded from the amalgamation of two local clubs in 1903. Aberdeen can sometimes appear so remote from any mainstream that outmoded ideas arrive there as novelties. Just when every major Scottish football team (Celtic, Hearts etc) has abandoned the idea of an out-of-town stadium, those governing AFC swallow the idea. A new ground is to be built at Loirston, south of the city, with a capacity of 25,000 when the Dons struggle to attract 10,000 supporters. This is despite the fact that local authority funding – initially promised – has been withdrawn. Pittodrie is walkable for many supporters, Loirston (with no station) depends on road links, ie, traffic jams, pollution etc, etc. This could be an albatross round the club's neck, one which could threaten its very existence. Teams undoubtedly reflect their town and AFC are no exception. It took the Dons over 50 years before they won the Scottish League in 1955, yet the canny directors paid a dividend in almost every year till then, even during the 1930s Depression. When Alex Ferguson came to Pittodrie in the 1980s

Glory Days for the Dons
They will never return, so why not have a look at this momento from Gothenburg in 1983? I can still recite the team from Gothenburg – and the one which won the League in 1955.

and asked for money for new players he was reputedly told by chairman Dick Donald, '*Na, na, Alex, ye'll jist hae tae makk dae wi the eens ye hiv gotten.*' The team that won the European Super Cup in 1983 was built for £750,000.

The fans are funny too. In 1955 the Dons won the League on 9 April at Clyde; their last home game was on 23 April. Their average home attendance that season was 15,000, yet only 10,000 turned up (and thus paid) to see the returned champions. I was one of the 10,000, though I hadn't paid as my dad had lifted me over the turnstiles to avoid the 9d entrance fee (it was 1s 6d for him). I have no footballing memories at all of that season but I do recall that what struck me was the overpowering smell of cigarette smoke and cloth caps and cloth coats, and urine mixed with cinders at the back of the brae leading down from the terraces. They are largely an undemonstrative lot, these Dons fans, and sometimes Pittodrie can be so quiet that the seagulls on the stand roof at the Beach End make more noise than the crowd. In the halcyon days of success in the 1980s crowds increased as did the levels of noise and exuberance, but in these times lassitude has returned. In football, as in most things, Aberdonians are not given to unrestrained enthusiasm. The fans have even been known to politely clap the opposing team. Like granite, they are solid, difficult to move and undemonstrative. Funnily enough, the Dons' away support is more boisterous.[2]

Pittodrie lies, or rather lay, in the area which was the heart of Aberdeen's granite industry, and virtually the last granite operation left today operates out of Merkland Road East, a couple of hundred yards from Pittodrie's main gates. From here southwards to Park Street and Constitution Street and on the streets off King Street lay many of the scores of granite works that flourished in Aberdeen at the industry's height.

> At one time all the one side of King Street was granite works, there were about eight or nine of them... We used to walk along King Street an you would see them at lunchtime with all those little cuts like a drunk man had been shavin. It wis the

men hittin the granite an the chips flyin up... they didnae hae safety goggles or gloves. You'd say 'Oh, this is a bloke fae the granite yards,' it was sae obvious.

Work, Welfare and the Price of Fish

The cutting and polishing of granite was a slow process even when mechanised, and machinery often ran night and day. Ashie Brebner who grew up in Seaforth Road, in the middle of this area, told me that his childhood had the low chug-chug of the mechanical saws as a constant accompaniment. Most of these works lay close to the railway line, built over the old Aberdeenshire canal, which gave access to the docks and the quarries of rural Aberdeenshire. For although 19th century Aberdeen was built from granite, a vast amount of the stone was exported either as building material or road material. The streets of London were not paved with gold, but with Aberdeen setts. Like all of the city's industries apart from paper and textiles, the granite industry was small scale; in 1900 the largest firm employed only 100 workers out of a total of 2,500 in the entire industry at that time, and the average unit had a labour force of about 30. You might expect that this would have led – as it did in both shore- and sea-based sides of the fishing industry – to a form of Victorian sweatshop capitalism, but the reality was rather different. Granite workers were real aristocrats of labour in a booming industry with insatiable demand for a high-quality and high-price product. A large proportion of the workers were skilled and had early success in establishing trade unions, which in turn got them high wages and advances in working conditions. By 1913 they had established a 44 hour week, 10 hours less than skilled workers in the local shipyards for example. It might be thought this was achieved by industrial action, but in reality the industry saw few strikes in its heyday, though it should be noted that the 44 hour week in 1913 was achieved through strike action.

The only long and bitter strike the industry ever saw was a 14-week-long one in 1955 over attempts by the employers to destroy the craft basis of the industry, which was by then in steep decline. Before that the attitude of the workers was expressed in 1905 by the Operative

Masons' and Granite Cutters' Union, which spoke of 'the peaceful policy which we have always pursued and ardently wish to pursue in the future... We have neither the desire nor the intention to do anything which will unfairly hamper or harass the employers.'

The workers also had other techniques to maintain their skill and wage levels. When the trade was slack in the winter months, due to the decline in building work, hundreds of granite masons would go across to various parts of the USA, especially to Vermont, in order to prevent a potential labour surplus which employers might abuse to force down wages. Additionally, in times of real slump the trade unions would give their members money to go overseas for longer periods and thus maintain the labour market equilibrium. Some of the workers even emigrated seasonally to Australia, working on the building of the Sydney Harbour Bridge. An amazing example, in the era of steamships, of the medieval tramping artisan.

The employers had granted the closed shop to granite workers in return for a commitment to compulsory arbitration. In return the workers agreed not to work for employers not registered with the employers' organisation. Also, to discourage competition, prohibitive entrance fees to the employers' organisation were charged. The employers also established a cartel to control the purchase of granite. These deals got employers continuous production and limited competition, and the workers good wages and conditions, but in the long run this cosy relationship kept the industry small-scale and was one cause of its ultimate demise. All the technological innovations of the later 19th century, for example power hand tools and polishing machinery, were developed in America, not Aberdeen. Amongst the other factors in the industry's decay were the increasing costs of quarrying and working the material, leading to the end of its use for house building from the 1950s. By then there were less than 1,500 granite workers.

There are very few locations where the former granite works can be viewed, as they were built over or converted for other uses. But in the vicinity of King Street we can see the end product of much of their labours in that the streets around Pittodrie and to the south contain some of the best extant versions of the Aberdeen working class tenement. In particular the fine sweep of Urquhart Road and its feeder streets have hardly changed externally in a century, though the interiors have been extensively re-modelled and upgraded. Many of these buildings were constructed in the late 1890s, and were the first municipal housing in Aberdeen. Tenements are a much maligned institution – usually by those who have never lived in them. But these modest tenements, even in their pre-improvement days, without baths and with shared toilets on the landings, gave better housing than the overcrowded pre-industrial lands and wynds of central Aberdeen. Critics called them 'granite rabbit hutches' and it is true that rooms were smaller and ceilings lower than, for example, in the Glasgow working class tenements of that time. Similarly sanitation standards were basic, with communal toilets on the landing, whereas in Glasgow, a by-law of 1891 had ensured that henceforth all tenements were constructed with toilets inside the flats.

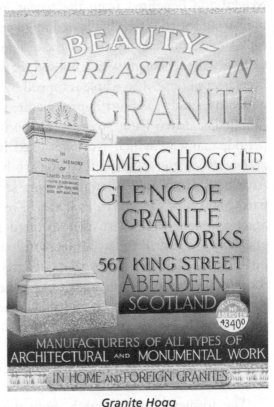

Granite Hogg
A beautiful example of the monumental granite work produced by Aberdeen's skilled granite masons. Nearly worth dying for.

Granite was not only used for building work, since it also came to almost monopolise the local monumental trade. A good place to see the products of the skilled monumental masons is St Peter's Cemetery on King Street just across from its junction with Merkland

Road East. And on gaining King Street, a whole cavalcade of fine granite buildings can be studied on the way back to the Castlegate. The first is what everyone in Aberdeen over 40 knows as the Corporation Bus Depot, but which was originally built as the Militia Barracks in the 1860s (at the same time as the Torry Battery), when fear of a French invasion led to an outburst of volunteering. It has crow-stepped gables and turrets as a reference to the wonderful fortified house architecture of the North East, exemplified in, for example, Craigievar Castle.

A couple of hundred yards down King Street on the eastern side stands the former fire station built in the 1890s and one of the most elaborate granite buildings in the city. Its architect, Arthur Mackinnon benefited from the recent introduction of hand power tools from the USA, which allowed more complex decoration of granite to be done more cheaply. Above the ornamented arches for the engines' exits, lies the tenement which housed the firemen, and to the left is the firemaster's house. The whole is topped by an Italianate fire-tower with a balcony, surely the most impressive fire station tower anywhere?

Further down King Street we come to buildings from an earlier period, many of which were designed by Aberdeen's two greatest architects of the first half of the 19th century, John Smith and Archibald Simpson. Whether it was lack of opportunity, or that parochialism of the North East which sees being a local hero as the highest honour, both these men operated in the city and surroundings only, and are denied the wider recognition that their genius demands. Luckily the planning blight that affected George Street, Aberdeen's other main thoroughfare which exits the city northwards, has not been visited on King Street, and this lower area contains a cluster of some of the finest buildings by this talented pair in the city. The reader/walker should consult WA Brogden's *Aberdeen: An Illustrated Architectural Guide* (1986), but some of the most notable buildings can be mentioned.

The former North Church, now the Aberdeen Arts Centre, is possibly Smith's masterpiece, with its dramatic portico of ionic columns facing northwards and the Greek-influenced tower above.

Grimsby Chambers, Harbour Area

Fine tenement building from the early 20th century, with elaborate granite balustrades. In good condition, unlike most of the other buildings in Aberdeen's waterfront area.

Tivoli Theatre

Aberdeen's Victorian Music Hall. Note the Romanesque arches above the doors and windows and the granite pillars at the entrances. In a depressing state of disrepair and neglect. Rumours are now rife about restoration plans.

Shore Porters' Society Warehouse

The oldest company in the world, still a co-operative. This warehouse is located in an early 19th century building by the harbour. Nowadays the SPS is a long distance haulage concern.

Fisher Houses, Auld Torry

Built for inshore fishermen before the days of trawling. Most were demolished for oil-related developments, but these brightly painted cottages from the later 18th century remain.

Trawler Painting

Proletarian artists are rare. The fish market porter Alexander Harwood attempted
to paint all the trawlers operating out of Aberdeen in the inter-war period.
Here is the *Barbara Robb*.
Courtesy of Aberdeen Maritime Museum.

Victoria Road, Torry

Still a busy place. Note that the top floor flats are built into the roof. These attics gave
canny Aberdonian builders an extra floor at little cost, four storeys for the price of
three, but the attic flats were even more cramped than the floors below.

Torry Fish Quine

Not too pleased at being photographed. The conditions in which she is working would have seemed like paradise up to the late 1960s, when 'fish-hooses' were insanitary hell holes, as described in Stanley Robertson's books of that name.

Education, Education, Education

The place where your author started his educational development. A building to put the fear of death in you, if not from the teachers, then from the jannie – Walker Road Primary School.

Fittie Tenement

One of the last few houses in an area that once supported two primary schools and a secondary. Most were demolished for industrial and warehousing developments. The pub remains – as do several others – as fowk still work in Fittie.

Harbour Master's Station

At Pocra Quay. Note the glorious *cassies*. Behind, across the River Dee, can be seen the oil storage facilities which replaced Auld Torry. Auld Fittie is still there, though, and well worth a stroll.

Fittie Shipyard Building

The former engine shop of Hall Russell's shipyard, long one of Aberdeen's biggest employers. Most of the yard was demolished and re-developed for the oil industry, but this building remains.

Well of Spa and Simpson's City Hospital

This was one of the main sources of the public water supply in Gilcomston when Willie Thom, the weaver bard, lived here. By Thom's days Gilcomston was a squalid slum of pre-industrial housing.

Rosemount Square

Not a square, despite the name, but one of Aberdeen's most unique buildings, based on the socialist models of town planning current in Berlin and Vienna between the wars. Note the Art Deco sculpture above the arched entrance.

Dark Satanic Mill?

The tower and lum of Broadford's textile factory rise above the red brick, caught in glorious sunshine, like some Italian hill town. But not such a pleasant place to work in, as it was to look at, *or so mi mither telt me.*

Tenements, Rosemount Viaduct

Marvellous, externally impressive buildings from the 1890s, but they had outside toilets, small rooms and were densely populated. But far better than the pre-industrial slums of Gilcomston over which they towered.

Northern Hotel, Kittybrewster

Art Deco 1930s hotel influenced by the ocean liner design of the period – and bearing more than a passing resemblance to the contemporary Rosemount Square? Recently refurbished after a period of decline.

Haudagain Retail Park

A pretty characterless development at the northern end of Woodside, with this unit unlet. It is on the site where travelling people lived, and there was a shanty-town in the 1930s.

Castlegate (the Castler)

Showing the Salvation Army Citadel and the Mercat Cross. John Paton did his early propaganda work for the Labour Party here, and it was later a favourite patch with Communist activists between the wars.

Woodside Tenements

Burnished in the sun, these splendid red granite tenements are unusual for Aberdeen, where they were usually grey. Note again the attic flats, where even chimney space is adapted for a room.

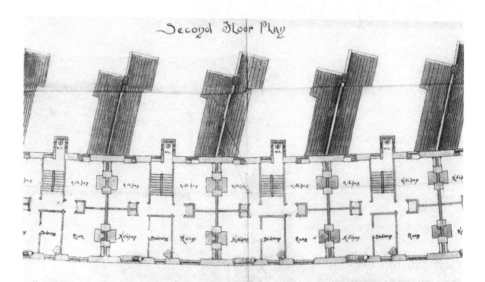

Second Floor Plan

First Floor Plan

Interior Plan of Urquhart Road Tenements

The Corporation's first council housing. On each floor there are three houses. One had a kitchen/living room only, one a kitchen/living room and small bedroom, the other a kitchen/living room and a larger room. All three shared one toilet on the landing.

Courtesy of Aberdeen City Archives.

Pittodrie Stadium

It seemed impressive to me when I was a boy, but I have to admit the entrance to
Pittodrie Stadium is a rather cheapskate piece of granite architecture. AFC directors
were never keen on spending money, as any Dons fan will tell you.

Monumental Granite Works

The last operating granite works in the city, in Merkland Road East. An industry
that paved the streets of London with *cassies*, and gave Aberdeen its built
character and its sobriquet, Granite City.

King Street Fire Station

Mackinnon's building was more elaborate than previous granite buildings
because of the new power carving tools introduced from the USA. Note
the city coat of arms atop, and the arched doors for the fire engines' exit.
The building is now residential.

Smith also built much of the housing on the east side of King Street, all of which is interesting and varied, although the middle classes for whom these dwellings were initially built soon moved out and they became overcrowded. This eastern side is possibly the best place to look across to Simpson's Medico-Chirurgical Building of 1818 in a severe classical mould, and his County Records office next to it. But the best is kept till last, Simpson's 1842 building for the North of Scotland Bank on the Union Street/King Street corner, often described as the Hinge of the City. The curved corner with its Corinthian columns echoes the 'hinge' theme. Giles' statue of Ceres sits on top, and inside, despite its conversion to a pub, much of the original interior remains, including a gilt Parthenon frieze, which is most impressive. In honour of the architect, the pub is named Archibald Simpson's.

We are back at the Castler. Even the virtual-reality *coortin* we have done at the fleshpots of the beach, the football supporting at Pittodrie, and thinking about the labours of the granite workers is hungry and drouthy work. If pub grub in Archibald Simpson's is not to your taste you could cross back over to the Castler and see if there is *ony taglatelly the day* in *La Lombarda*.

Notes

1   An obvious choice of a statue for the Castler would be one of Cocky
    Hunter, the trader mentioned above. However after much debate a
    decision has been made to erect – elsewhere – a new statue in
    Aberdeen, one in traditional mould, of... Robert the Bruce! What
    inspiration! What imagination!

2   A friend commented on reading this, '*Aiberdeen fans are jist like
    granite, often grim but they can sparkle.*' A non-Aberdonian might
    take this as a literal assertion, which is disagreeing with my view of
    the dour Pittodrie faithful. Rather it is a piece of typically understated
    Aberdonian humour (so understated outsiders often miss it) which is
    actually *confirming* my view. For the idea of a Dons supporter – or
    any Aberdonian for that – 'sparkling' is preposterous.

CHAPTER FIVE

Haudagain tae Kittybrewster

WOODSIDE IS NOT AN AREA of Aberdeen that attracts a great deal of attention, and some of the attention it does get can be negative. In his *Aberdeen: An Illustrated Architectural Guide,* WA Brogden describes Woodside as 'alas, not a happy place now'. And it is true that much of Woodside and its adjacent areas do not appear to the casual eye to have shared in the oil boom prosperity of some other parts of Aberdeen. However, 'fae Kittybrewster tae Haudagain' (which are respectively the southern and northern boundaries of Woodside) takes us through one of the city's most interesting areas. Woodside has a geographical coherence, an interesting historical built environment, a unique industrial history and a collection of local characters that give it a real local identity.

Woodside owes its existence to the Industrial Revolution. Till well after 1750 there was little there, and one observer of that time described the area as covered by 'black heath which came close to the town'. But by 1800 the fast-flowing waters of the River Don provided power for the establishment at Woodside of the largest concentration of textile manufacture north of Lanarkshire. Until 1850, 25 per cent of Aberdeen's population, a total of 13,000 workers, worked in textiles and many of the largest mills were at Woodside. Robert Duncan's fine short pamphlet *Textiles and Toil* (1984) gives a picture of the time when Woodside and Aberdeen looked well on the way to becoming a northern Bolton or Paisley.

In 1785 Gordon Barron and Co. founded the Woodside Mill, which at its peak employed 3,000 workers making cotton. Some of the workers were brought from Derbyshire to operate the new textile machinery. In the 1790s Leys, Masson and Co.'s Grandholm Mill opened across the river and by 1817 4,000 workers were engaged in linen manufacture there. Just along the river lay Gordon's Mills, where another 1,000 workers laboured, as they all did then, a six-day week of 72 hours work, for between five and 10 shillings.

Woodside's prosperity was secured when the Aberdeen to Inverurie canal was constructed through it in 1805, giving direct access to the harbour of the city. Much of the textile industry was heavily dependant on imported raw materials and its mass production needed a large export market. The canal was later bought and closed by the Great North of Scotland Railway, which filled it in and built a railway line along its length to the harbour in 1855. Later a passenger line was constructed out from Guild Street Station to Woodside via the Denburn. This line ran local services to stations at Kittybrewster, Don Street, Woodside and Persley, which continued into the 1930s when they closed due to the competition of the Corporation tram-lines. Woodside thus was well-served by four stations on the suburban line, or 'subbies' as they were called. My father was brought up in Woodside and remembers the subbies with affection, partly because he knew the station masters and could fare-dodge. Most accounts say the trams were cheaper (and more frequent), but my dad says it was people's laziness that killed the subbies. '*Ye hidnae sae far tae wakk wi the trams.*'

The expansion of the railway system in the North East in the 1850s and '60s meant that Woodside also partly became a railway town for a while, when the largest rail repair and manufacture facility north of the Central Belt was opened at Kittybrewster in 1855. This locomotive works serviced all of the Great North of Scotland Railway lines radiating from Aberdeen to Inverness, Deeside and Buchan, until it was transferred out to Inverurie in 1902.

The economic crisis of 1848 wiped out much of Aberdeen and Woodside's textile industry, leaving mainly specialised niche producers. The Woodside Mill and Gordon's Mills closed their doors, and Grandholm survived by switching to high-quality woollens produc-tion after being acquired by Crombie and Sons in 1859. The crisis in textiles meant Woodside's population actually fell after 1850, only reaching the same level again in 1880. But a new industry helped fill the gap: paper making. The Woodside Mill was bought by Pirie's paper manufacturers and in 1888, after lying idle for many years, Gordon's Mills were converted to the new product, trading as the Donside Paper Company from 1893. Other paper mills were opened just north of Woodside, at Mugiemoss and a little further out at Stoneywood, which meant that the lost textile work was to a large extent replaced by that from paper making. Today Stoneywood is the only paper mill still in production. The work in the paper industry was higher paid and the working conditions were better than in the textile mills. Woodside thus retained the atmosphere of a mill town and increasing population allowed it to become a police burgh in 1868, before the town and surrounding areas were annexed by an expanding Aberdeen in 1891, and it had about 20,000 inhabitants in 1914.

A good place to start an exploration of Woodside is at the so-called Wallace Tower on the edge of Seaton Park. This building has nothing to do with William Wallace, who is not the armed figure on its wall (this was added a century after the building was built any-way) and neither was the Tower built here. Benholm's Lodging, as it was originally called, is a small fortified 17th century house which lay in central Aberdeen and was moved to its current location in the 1960s to facilitate a new city centre shopping development. This involved the creation of an ugly arcade which blocked Union Street off from George Street and turned the latter thoroughfare into a neglected and run down canyon. However, few can deny that the Tower adds to the drama of the scene in its new location, as the Don flows past through wooded slopes, towards the solid spires of St Machar's Cathedral. Though it was heavily industrial, lower Donside remained and still is a beautiful place. It is a pity the Tower is boarded up, empty and sub-ject to vandalism.

The site of Gordon's Mills cotton works, which later became that of the Donside Paper Company, lies just below the Tower. The name of the works is recalled in Gordon's Mills Road, which leads us upriver from the Tower. In fact this street name long predates the textile, and indeed paper, industry. Robert Gordon of Straloch's map *Aberdonia & Banfia* of 1654 shows Gordon's Mill in exactly this spot, though at that time it was probably a meal mill. At the end of Don Terrace a set of steps leads you down to the river. Opinions to the number of steps in the flight would appear to vary, but I counted 99. Its name however, is well-established, and not in dispute: Jacob's Ladder. Presumably, Heaven to the weary mill workers lay at the top of these steps after the day's toil.

At the top of the steps is a rather sad sign pointing down to Grandholm Mills; for the last 10 years the works has been closed. For 200 years thousands of men and women took these steps, then crossed the private mill bridge to work in the factory, reversing the process at the end of a hard day. Most of the mill has been demolished and turned into a middle class housing estate. This factory made high-quality woollens for the Confederate Army in the US Civil War, for the British Army in the two World Wars and even for the Red Army and KGB higher echelons prior to the demise of the Soviet Union. When I was young, many respectable working men of the older generation had a Crombie coat for ceremonial occasions: weddings, funerals, football matches. But changing tastes killed off Grandholm (Grannam as it was locally called), though the firm still makes items for the luxury market from its Leeds factory. No more does the clatter of the wooden clogs of the mill workers against the granite *cassies* as they headed down Don Street towards Jacob's Ladder waken up the inhabitants of Woodside, as was described by Andrew McKessock of his child-hood days in *Woodside Ways*, published in 1977.

Grandholm was, as a woollen mill, a better place to work than the cotton mills with their bronchial dampness and the flax mills with their choking dust. Crombies were also paternalistic employers, offering sick pay and pension schemes at a time when these were scarce – but as with many such firms, the price of paternalism was low wages. The fine wee pamphlet *Fae A The Airts Tae Haudagain* describes the surprise of a women working at Grandholm in the 1930s, when she discovered that her friends in the paper mills at Stoneywood earned £5 a week, almost twice her own wage. An attempt to cut wages further in 1938 led to a dispute which saw the unionisation of Grandholm and the gradual improvement of wages there. 'They got aff wi murder at Grannam afore the union,' concluded

Grandholm Mills, Woodside
One of the many large textile factories that made Woodside a 19th century mill town. This particular works operated for almost two centuries, first as a linen factory and then as a quality woollens mill.

the interviewee. Another place they got off with murder was Mugiemoss paper mill, where even in the 1960s the owners successfully resisted trade union organisation amongst the production workers, and where wages and conditions compared unfavourably with the Stoneywood paper mill.

Industrial Donside in its heyday was not a place of 'dark Satanic mills'. In fact the fine granite of buildings like Grandholm enhanced the drama of the river setting, as old prints of Donside's factories show. Heading west from the former mill you enter the sylvan world of Persley Den, scene of Woodside *coorting* for generations. This is a deep glade, through which runs the Don and the Grandholm Lead, constructed to carry water to the mill – and Persley is a delightful collage of riverscape and woods. At the very entrance to the Den, but across the River Don, is a housing development, Mill Court. This was the site of the original Woodside Cotton Works. It later became an adjunct to Stoneywood paper mill, processing rags for high-quality paper before finally closing down in the 1950s.

Though the Woodside mill is gone, as are all of Woodside's textile factories, other buildings associated with the former works remain, as you find when you exit from Mill Lade Wynd and turn left briefly onto the A90 and then head southwards, meeting Mugiemoss Road. Off Mugiemoss Road, by the River Don, are to be found two interesting buildings associated with Woodside Works. Woodside House was the home of one of the chief investors in the Woodside cotton mill, Patrick Barron, whilst to the west of it is another building dating from 1797, variously known as The Castle or The Barracks. This was built as a home for orphans, destitute children and others, for example children from reformatories who were indentured as apprentices in the Woodside cotton works. Until the passage of the early Factory Acts in the 1830s, these bairns worked under conditions little different from slavery. Today both Woodside House and The Castle are residential homes for the elderly.

Great Northern Road is, or was, the main thoroughfare of Woodside, but its northern side was demolished in the 1970s to make way for a dual carriageway, meaning the street has lost much of the character it possessed in old photographs and in the minds of residents of Woodside, past and present. Walking back eastwards along the road, on the south side is the Haudagain retail park, a rather ugly assortment of small works and warehouses. This used to be the site of the Haudagain Inn on the main road north out of Aberdeen and later became the main place where Woodside's large travelling community lived, until they began to gain access to council housing. Across from Haudagain are modern blocks of medium-rise flats. My father told me that when he was a boy between the wars, there stood here Hardup Mansions, as the locals called a tenement building which housed some of the poorest of the local population.

Since the north side of Great Northern Road has been totally demolished, it is more instructive and pleasant to walk along its southern pavement. In fact, if you are seeking refreshment you could do worse than I did by stopping at Fergie's Café, where I had pea soup and stovies of great excellence and incredible cheapness. Fergie's is the best café in Woodside, indeed the only one, and I don't think it gets many non-local customers. It was school lunch break and, to honour the presence of a visitor who they probably guessed was '*a chiel amang theem takkin notes*', the local bairns there with their *mithers* were getting copious clouts on the lugs and being told to behave. '*Dinna pick up yer peece fae the fleer, even if ye are fae Widside,*' yelled one outraged matron at her offspring. I was reluctant to leave but had to capture some of Woodside's architectural gems before the winter sun got too low in the sky.

Woodside New Parish Church's clock tower lies just off Great Northern Road; it is visible from all over Woodside, so it's the area's main landmark. The kirk was built by the Aberdeen architect Archibald Simpson in the late 1840s. By this time the original Woodside Parish Church, dating from 1829 and also designed by Simpson, had become the Free Kirk. Today the latter is converted into flats; the former is still in use. Simpson was a great friend of the painter James Giles, who painted his portrait, and together the friends formed the first Aberdeen Artists' Society. Giles was one of Aberdeen's best 19th century painters, with his mountain landscapes and depictions of castles favoured by such as Queen Victoria. He was born in Woodside in 1801 and his father was a calico block printer in the Woodside cotton mill. Just along from the Simpson kirks lies the Anderson Library, built in the 1880s from the benefactions of Sir John Anderson, a local man who started as an engineer in the Woodside cotton works and later became production manager of the Woolwich Arsenal. Anderson was responsible for much innovation in the design and production of weapons, which made him very rich. The library holds a small collection of books and other materials on local history.

Further on again, Don Street joins Great Northern Road. Here for generations was the 'cross' of Woodside, the hub of the community where stood the much-loved fountain. Now, it wasn't all that much of a fountain, just a trough for the horses at the original tram terminus, with a lamppost attached to it. But it was a focal point. People met and courted there and kids played around it, no doubt chanting some of the street songs I later heard from my father, such as:

> Mathew, Mark, Luke and John
> Haud the cuddy ere I get on
> Haud it siccar, haud it sair
> Haud it by the heid o hair.

The Fountain was also an open-air rallying point for political meetings. In 1937 attempts by Fascists to organise a meeting here were broken up by local people and eight demonstrators arrested and fined. When the road was widened, the fountain disappeared, despite the fact that there was ample room to re-erect it here. Only the Fountain Bar tells of the former location of the landmark.

Down Don Street was Canal Street and the bridge across the railway that led to Grandholm. Canal Street was where my father grew up. My father's father was a labourer in the goods station in central Aberdeen, and low-paid. His was a small family for the time, with 'only' four children, and they lived in a two-room house with outside toilet, where heating and cooking were from a kitchen range. Grandma Mitchell was long dead before I went to 'Canallie' as it was termed, and Grandpa Mitchell was a quiet old man I never really knew. I later discovered he had been gassed at Ypres in World War One. The houses in Canallie were some of the worst in Woodside and have long since been demolished. But even the inhabitants of Canallie were favoured compared to those living in a couple of fields near Haudagain in 1936. The fields were let to various tenants living in tents and self-constructed shacks; there was no water on site and the area was rat infested.

Woodside appears to have had other exotic forms of housing. Mike Dey told me:

> There were prefabs at Hayton, opposite the Donside Mill; these were a great boon for working class families and gave an inside bathroom/toilet with even a gas fridge provided and gardens. There were also at Hayton, close by the prefab site, wartime huts which at the end of the war briefly contained families (including me); this was at a time when squatting was

ongoing in parts of the city. Occupation of these huts was done with official sanction and organisation and, I was told, helped gain a front-door key to the new prefabs.

Squatting appears to have been a much more widespread tactic of housing struggle in Aberdeen than elsewhere and its history cries out for a proper investigation.

Huge changes took place in Woodside between the wars of the last century, when the Powis estate round about it was developed for council housing as part of the slum clearance programme. Though all these houses were a major improvement on what went before, some were better designed than others and much of the new Woodside consisted of austere barrack-like buildings, which by the 1950s were seen as undesirable, and therefore let to unskilled, low-paid workers or so-called problem families, such as travelling people.

The hard angularity of some of the 1920s and '30s council housing in Woodside can be seen in Printfield Terrace, just south off Great Northern Road as we continue past the site of the former Fountain. Here at No. 6, during World War Two, was born Scotland's greatest-ever football player – Dennis Law. In his autobiography *The King* Law tells of his upbringing until he

From Canal Street to the Suez Canal
A 'Canallie *loon*' with a German tank captured single-handedly at El Alamein *(I think that's fit he telt mi fan I wis wee)*. After the war my father was secretary of the Gordon Highlanders' Association, so a lot of folk *kent mi faither*.

left the city in the mid-1950s. His father was a trawler deck-hand whom he hardly knew and who, like many 'deckies', drank Saturday, slept Sunday and went to sea Monday to Friday. The family was poor, Law says, and like others at the time, they had no carpets, no fridge, no central heating. He owned his first pair of shoes at 14, his mother (not alone locally in this attitude) being too proud to take the free school boots on offer, and he spent his winters in wellingtons and his summers in 'gymmies' (gym shoes). At that time Printfield Terrace was an improvement for the large Law family, who moved there in the 1930s from a house with an outside toilet.

But a much greater improvement for those cleared from the slums would have been the houses further up the brae, in Hilton, where the four-in-a-block with garden front and back council housing was reserved for the council's 'better' tenants. Here, in Hilton Drive, lived my maternal grandparents. My grandfather, a first mate on the trawlers, had a small First World War Navy pension. I first went to this house in the 1950s, when only my grandparents lived there. Many years later I realised that this desirable Home for Heroes, of two bedrooms, kitchen, bathroom and living room, had been occupied by two adults and *seven* children in the 1930s. I was closer to my maternal than paternal grandparents. I could never understand why *Grunnie* spoke Doric with a funny accent; later of course I realised that she had been speaking Geordie, which had many similar words to Doric. Granda Henderson was an interesting man, who was amongst the earliest supporters of the Labour Party in Scotland, like fellow *Lossie loon*, Ramsay MacDonald – though he (Granda) briefly voted Communist in the 1930s. He was also a strong union man and this meant that he was never able to use his skipper's ticket on the trawlers: skippers were not union men.

Conscripted to mine-sweeper work in both World Wars, his boat was sunk in each conflict. Despite being, like almost all fishermen, unable to swim, he survived both sinkings. 'Grumpy' as we called him was very proud that his eldest son later became the head of the Fisheries section of the Transport and General Workers' Union. He was a man of many couthy and wise statements, more of which I wish I had recorded. One I do recall was, *'Ye growe like the fowk ye bide wi.'* In my first year at university I discovered that this was the principle of socialisation, the basis of all sociology. I was also astonished to discover that many of the words I came across in Chaucer's *Canterbury Tales* were ones my grandfather used, learned in his Lossie childhood: *wyte*, for example, and *himnest*. He died before I could communicate any of this to him. (On linguistic matters, next door was old Mrs MacRobbie, with a voice like a strangled hen and the most amazing line in malapropisms. For her smoke went up a 'lumney' and you made calls from a 'telephone cossack'.)

One of my grandparents' near neighbours was Jeannie Robertson, the great Aberdeenshire ballad singer and traveller, who lived in Hilton Road. I was later privileged to see her perform many times in Aberdeen when she achieved due and belated fame beyond the travelling community and amongst academic ethnologists, in the 1960s. But let's get back doon the brae to Woodside proper. On the northern side of Great Northern Road lies the district of Ferrier Crescent and Sandilands Drive. Jeannie was lucky to get a house in Hilton. Most travelling people and other 'problem' tenants were deposited by Aberdeen council in these streets, which was the nearest the Granite City formerly had to an urban ghetto. Today it has if anything worsened since boarded-up and burnt-out houses... in the energy capital of Europe. Yet just across Great Northern Road from here are a line of tenements which I would rate amongst the finest in the city, in immaculate order. They are unusual in their mixing of pink and grey granite which gives a wonderful dappled effect.

South from Sandilands is Kittybrewster, where the old GNSR workshops were located on the area now occupied by a large trading and industrial estate. From the roundabout here you can go back down St Machar Drive, past the secondary school of that name, and take Tillydrone Avenue back to the Wallace Tower, or you can proceed further into deepest Kittybrewster. Where Great Northern Road joins Clifton Road, you will come to one of Aberdeen's best inter-war buildings, the A-listed art deco Northern Hotel, whose balconied façade is shaped like a ship's stern.

Originally a stylish resort, this hotel sank over time into a disreputable hard-drinking place. In recent years it has been restored to much of its former glory, however. The Kittybrewster Bar may also be a tempting port of call at this point. And after some refreshment, you may well decide to *haudagain tae Widside* in future.

CHAPTER SIX

Roon Aboot Rosemount

GEORGE WASHINGTON WILSON WAS Aberdeen's (and Scotland's) most famous 19th century photographer, but he was first a painter, and he continued to draw and paint after his photographic fame was established. In 1850 Wilson drew a bird's-eye view of Aberdeen looking north from the town centre, followed by another almost 40 years later. These give a unique image of the growth of the city in the period of its most rapid expansion.

In the first picture Rosemount does not exist, apart from a few middle class suburban villas and rural cottages, separated from Aberdeen by green fields. By 1889, the entire area between city and suburbs has been filled in, to a great extent by the expansion of working class tenement properties. As WA Brogden says in his *Aberdeen: An Illustrated Architectural Guide*, 'Rosemount is an excellent place to observe the Aberdeen tenement.' It is that, but it is much more, having many interesting buildings from the pre- and post-tenement periods, as well as significant sections of middle class housing, making it architecturally a more complex district than the others discussed in this work.

Rosemount starts just outside the city centre, where the impressive line of Rosemount Viaduct sweeps northwards. Here stand some of the finest and most original of Aberdeen's tenements, in clean and solid granite, built from the late 1870s through to about 1900. The best are probably No. 96–120 with their turrets and Gothic window decorations, and No. 1–27, with their curving design. These might appear to the untutored observer to be middle class dwellings, but the exterior grandeur belied the interiors, which were generally small units, and, initially, had outside toilets.

Dr Brogden, an American, is like many of his countrymen perplexed by our plumbing. He says of the Rosemount tenements, 'Why there should have been such a poor provision of plumbing is a mystery.' But granite is an expensive material to quarry, shape and build with, compared for example to sandstone or brick. The canny Aberdonian house builders could not economise on building materials, but they could, and did, on plumbing. And it was also possibly the cost of the building material which made the cubic volume of the tenements of the Aberdeen working class so restricted. On the other hand the high durability of granite ensured that, in regard to the later Victorian tenements, very few decayed in the way sandstone often did, and large numbers from that epoch remain. Slum clearance in Aberdeen in the 20th century meant that of largely pre- and early industrial dwellings.

However the most interesting building hereabouts, indeed in the whole of Rosemount and possibly in Aberdeen itself, is not a tenement, but one which is quite unique for Scotland. Rosemount Square was started in 1938 and finished after the war in 1945. The 'square' is actually on the inside of the block, which is formed on its exterior in the shape of an oblong with a curved south end. This building was designed as an imitation of the blocks of workers' apartments (*Arbeiterhofe*) put up in Vienna between the wars by the socialist administration, and this one recalls the *Karl Marx Hof* in that city. The building is also enriched by wonderful Art Deco sculptures, the *Spirits of the Wind and Rain* by Huxley-Jones, above the entrance arches. Rosemount Square was identified in a 1999 Church of Scotland survey as one of the most deprived areas in the city, though everything is relative and when walking around it, I have felt that most inhabitants of Possil or Govan in my adoptive Glasgow would give an arm and a leg to live here. How did Aberdeen come to have such a unique building? It was designed by the City Architect's office under AB Gardner, at a time when the Housing Convenor was the noted local architect and town planner T Scott Sutherland. Now, Sutherland was a Conservative and unlikely (though he actually named Rosemount Square) to have had any sympathy for socialist models of town planning. If any reader can enlighten me about this building, I would be delighted to hear from them[1].

Carrying on uphill past Rosemount Square we come to

Rosemount Place, the social and shopping heart of Rosemount. Turning right you drop down Rosemount Place to Skene Square (which, like Rosemount Square, isn't a square either, but a straight street; Rosemount's geometry is very non-Euclidean!). Rosemount Place is mainly a late 19th century development, but behind the tenements there used to be many pre-industrial buildings. One which survives behind 28 Rosemount Place is the lovely Regency Rosemount House, now modern flats. It is well worth seeing.

Rosemount was never really a predominantly industrial area, although there were some granite works in its southern reaches. But here on its eastern boundaries, across Skene Square, lay for over two centuries one of the most important factories in Aberdeen, Broadford's Linen Works in Maberly Street. Broadford's was unusual for Aberdeen in that it was developed by an outsider, Thomas Maberly, an English capitalist and also an MP. When his firm collapsed in 1830, Richards and Co. became the owners, and remained so till the works finally closed in the early years of this century. The Broadford's complex of buildings in Maberly Street is also unusual for Aberdeen in the amount of brick used in its construction, notably the huge turreted and castellated raw materials store. This, with its prominent position, was an eye-catching landmark from all directions during the years of its operation. It was famed as a building without windows, and I was pleased to see that in its conversion to flats, sensitive fenestration befitting the building had been inserted. To the north of the flax store lies the former mill itself, a handsome construction of mixed granite and brick, hopefully awaiting a new use rather than demolition. The whole site is A-listed, which should help matters.

Even for the early industrial period Broadford's was notorious for its harsh treatment of the workforce, mainly teenage women and boys. Broadford's saw the first large-scale strike action undertaken in Aberdeen when around 1,000 women left their machines in 1834. They demanded higher wages and formed a union, the Female Operative Union. Though they won their wage claim, the union was broken and many subsequently victimised female mill girls used the last of the strike funds to take themselves to Dundee to look for work. The excellent pamphlet, *Textiles and Toil* by Rob Duncan, produced by Aberdeen City Libraries back in 1984, gives much interesting information on Broadford's and the early industrial period in Aberdeen. There were further strikes at Broadford's in 1901 and 1910–11, when workers were again sacked for joining trade unions. It was not until the 1930s that the Textile Workers Union gained a solid foothold in the factory, and latterly the union's offices were in Maberly Street. Also in Maberly Street was Maberly House, a boarding house owned by Maggie Rose, leader of the local Communist party. Our group of youthful anarchists waged war on the local Stalinist establishment and we had a verse, to the tune of 'Free Beer and Vodka for the Workers', which expressed our disapproval of how Maggie ran her capitalist boarding house enterprise:

> 'We'll makk Maggie Rose clean the stairs o Maberly Hoose
> (sung three times)
> When the Red Revolution comes along.'

Just over a century after the 1834 strike, my mother's first job after leaving school was in Broadford's. Professor Ian Richardson of Aberdeen University examined Broadford's works in the 1930s and described them thus:

> The working conditions were some of the poorest in Aberdeen. You only went there if you couldn't get anything else. I was shocked, it was like something out of the Dark Ages, out of the early industrial revolution.
> You could hardly see, it was like going into a dense fog (due to flax dust)... There was a lot of unguarded machinery...
>
> Quoted in *Work, Welfare and the Price of Fish*

As a result of Richardson's recommendations several improvements were made to safety in the works, but it remained the last resort for most job seekers in the city.

My mother talked of how glad she was to get a move from Broadford's to the Co-operative Dairy in nearby Berryden Road. A unique feature of the *dyree* was its huge glass windows through which you could watch the bottling process in operation. The *dyree* was cleaner and less arduous work, undertaken for a few years before wartime service, and then marriage placed her in the domestic situation towards which most Aberdonian married women gravitated. Working class respectability in the city meant earning enough to support a housewife, and Aberdeen always had far fewer married women in its work-force than other Scottish places.

A cluster of *Copey* (as it is locally designated) enterprises were situated here in Berryden and latterly when they went the way of most Co-op industrial units into oblivion, it became the site of the Norco superstore. Aberdonian parochialism is proverbial; it is the Catalonia of Caledonia. Just as, for example, the Cairngorm Club remained jealously separate from the Scottish Mountaineering Club, so too did the Northern Co-operative Society stand aloof from the scws. Since the Northern Co-op paid a higher *divvi* than the scws, the members of the *Copey* probably didn't mind. At the south end of this area is Cooney Court, social housing which commemorates Bob Cooney, a leading Communist activist of the 1930s and International Brigade member. Much information about Cooney and other local Aberdeen Brigaders is to be found in *Homage to Caledonia* by Daniel Gray, recently published by Luath Press.

Leaving the formerly industrial area around Maberly Street, you approach the splendid Rosemount Kirk which tells you that you are entering a different world. This

The Copay and the Divvi

Like many other North East institutions the local co-operative association held aloof from the Scottish organisation. The Northern Co-op had the highest rate of membership, and the highest dividend, in the country. *Wi the biggest divvi and the cheapest gas, the place wis near tae Paradise.*

church was built in 1875 by William Smith, the architect of Balmoral Castle no less, and in Westburn Road we are definitely in a quality residential district. Middle class Rosemount retained its character, despite losing its suburban status in the later 19th century, and remains today a most pleasant district. The social division in Rosemount between its working class part, south of Rosemount Place, and northern middle class segment is clear to the eye. On Rosemount Place, you have (generally) tenements on the south side, villas and cottages on the north. And within the area between Rosemount Place and Westburn Road there is a concentration of interesting architecture difficult to match elsewhere in Aberdeen.

Strolling along Westburn Road, you soon come to the Victoria Park on the left and the Westburn Park on the right, both finely laid out. In Westburn Park lies Westburn House, one of the best works of Archibald Simpson, the 'Architect of Aberdeen'. Though Simpson put his unique stamp on the Granite City in the first half of the 19th century, most of his work is found in the North East and he does not receive the Scotland-wide recognition he deserves. Westburn House was built in 1839 as a home for the proprietor of the *Aberdeen Journal*. The fine balustraded veranda was added later when the building was converted from domestic to park use. Sadly, on my last visit the A-listed Westburn House was boarded up; can Aberdeen with its oil money not do better than this?

Victoria Park was Aberdeen's first civic park, laid out at the rather late date of 1871. In it stands a unique structure, a fountain made of 14 different types of granite, donated to the park by the Granite Polishers and Master Builders of Aberdeen. Victoria Park also has a very interesting building, *Montarosa* at the south end of Thomson Street, overlooking the park. This was the home of local builder, civil engineer and businessman John Morgan, whose company constructed much of the finest housing in Aberdeen's West End. Morgan later moved further west to an even finer villa, Rubislaw House, in Queen's Road. On its western side Victoria Park is flanked by Argyll Place, a good example of 1870s town-planning, with middle class terraced villas rising up the brae in a fine sweep. In nearby

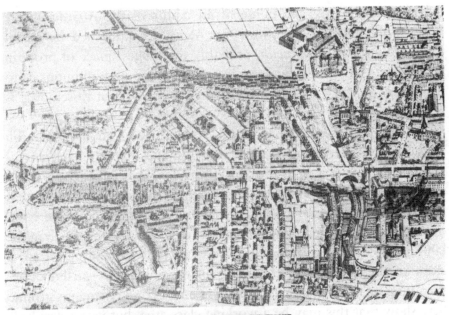

*Rosemount 1850
and 1889*
Washington Wilson's two
drawings show the
Rosemount area first as
the Gilcomston slum
surrounded by open
country, then as
tenements and villas
forty years later.

Belvidere Street was the home of an editor of the *Aberdeen Free Press*, William Alexander. In 1871 Alexander published his novel *Johnny Gibb of Gushetneuk*, probably the longest piece of prose in Scots since the Middle Ages. Its length is undisputed; opinions as to its literary quality vary. But the 'quality' of this part of Rosemount is not in dispute.

At the top, southern, end of Argyll Place you are back on Rosemount Place, from where it slowly makes its way back downhill. This street is a fine off-town-centre location, with good shops and little or no dereliction. In fact, I was surprised to see that Rosemount appears to becoming quite '*vif*' with fashionable retail outlets and cafés appearing. At Esslemont Avenue we are back in the land of tenements, and this street shows a fluid serpentine sweep of clean granite, rather marred however by the ubiquitous satellite dishes sprouting on their frontages. Other streets of good tenements around here show that this may be a working class area, but it is a decidedly 'respectable' one. If Aberdeen has an equivalent of Glasgow's Dennistoun, Rosemount is it.

Esslemont Avenue leads to the southern boundary of Rosemount, Skene Street. Many of the tenements hereabouts were demolished and the residents scooped up into the high rise blocks of flats on the south side of the street, but some interesting cameos remain of the architecture constructed when this was open country. Skene Place on the north side of the street, dating from the early 19th century, is a delight to the eye, with the segmental fan window above the double central entrance doors of the block. And if you drop down to the Denburn, where it flows free of the culverts that have largely made this watercourse invisible, a wonder awaits you. Mackie Place consists of a couple of mansions dating from around 1815, deep in the Denburn *haugh* and surrounded by trees. One can imagine the building when it stood, as it did for over half a century, in open countryside, with the Denburn flowing freely. In Mackie Place is also the last weaver's shed in the city. There were plans to develop it as an interpretive centre in the 1980s, but these came to nothing and it has since been left to deteriorate. This, along with the state of many other buildings, does seem to indicate a more than usual lack of concern in Aberdeen about its heritage and its past.

Just before the end of Skene Street are a set of stairs on the left, leading down to the Upper Denburn and Jack's Brae. Here you actually go underneath Rosemount Viaduct, into an area that existed before Rosemount and was absorbed by it, that of Gilcomston. Gilcomston used to be a location of the handloom weaving industry which flourished in Aberdeen till about 1850. Observers from the later 18th century provide an idyllic picture of Gilcomston ('this fine village') as the abode of prosperous weavers in a countryside location. But as industrialisation spread the area went downhill and in 1818 an observer said 'the buildings are mean and very irregular, many of them being occupied by labourers and the lower classes of the people'. The Denburn itself gradually became polluted by tanneries, breweries and textile works, leading to the local poet James Ogg addressing the Town Council in the name of the burn, as follows:

Wi sterlin sorrow I begin
This hamely blunt effusion
Gweed kens, respected sirs, I'm in
A state of sad pollution
Ugh! Up aside the Tannerie
I'm loathsome foul and muddy,
A truly shockin sicht tae see
By ony cleanlie bodie.

In parallel with this deterioration of the environment, from 1815 onwards the economic state of the handloom weavers became increasingly parlous, and they sank relentlessly into poverty and overwork.

Going under Rosemount Viaduct and negotiating your way round the Denburn Health Centre, you come to Spa Street, formerly a street of handloom weavers and one-time home of Willie Thom, the famous Aberdeen weaver-poet (see chapter 8). The whole of the pre-industrial village of pan-tiled weavers' cottages was swept away and replaced in the 19th century by tenements. Here, however, they were not generally of the quality found elsewhere in Rosemount, and in the 1960s Gilcomston was flattened and much of its population re-housed in the multi-story block which towers above the Denburn today.

One pleasing relic of the past which survives is the Well of Spa, used in Willie Thom's time as the public water supply, and before that famed as a medicinal well. No longer drawing water, it nevertheless stands proud in front of the multi-story block, slightly moved from its original location. Behind this, a possibly more reliable contribution to public health was Archibald Simpson's grand domed Aberdeen (later Royal) Infirmary, completed in 1839 to cater for the town's poor. At that time rich people tended to be treated at home.

Today, down in their hollow, Gilcomston folk tend to feel a bit separate from Rosemount. As if to emphasise this, a sign outside the Gilcomston Bar claims the antiquity of their settlement (with what accuracy I know not) as about 1,000 years, thus pre-dating Rosemount by just a little. The Well of Spa Bar, where I did my first underage drinking in the 1960s amongst *cairters* and coalmen, a clientele enlivened by quick visits from members of the orchestra from His Majesty's Theatre in the show's interval, dressed in all their finery, is no more. Across from the Well of Spa, a set of steps (Donald's Way) leads up past the side of HM Theatre and back to our starting point on Rosemount Viaduct. Rosemount is certainly an area in good heart, a far cry from negative inner city clichés, and it gives a rewarding couple of hours' off-city-centre ramble.

Notes

1 For the background to Rosemount Square, which was largely designed by Leo Dumin working under AB Gardiner, see Mark Chalmers, *Rosemount Square, Aberdeen; Modernism in Granite,* http//www.urbanrealm.com.

CHAPTER SEVEN

Kincorth: Nithing bit Hooses?

'*DAE THE KINKERS? It's nithing bit hooses,*' was my first reaction to the suggestion.

The working class residential areas which developed between the wars of the last century, and increasingly after 1945, were different from those that had come before. Generally built by the state, not by private contractors, they differed not only because they were constructed to a lower population density and with superior sanitation facilities – important though that was. Equally importantly, they were built separate from industry for health and environmental reasons. In many cases, because few facilities like shops, pubs and schools were originally built into them, these housing schemes could often accurately be described as '*nithing bit hooses*'.

The Kincorth housing scheme (like Torry it was '*owir the watter*' but additionally 'up the (Kincorth) hill') was planned before World War Two but laid out after it, from the later 1940s to the mid-60s. Many people who moved there – like my own family – were from Torry. This fact was marked by a curious transport phenomenon, distinct from the radial pattern of all other city bus routes: the Kincorth Circular. This went as the No. 15 in one circular direction on a Torry–Kincorth run, and as the No. 16 in the reverse clockwise direction, to take folk to their workplaces. The houses were well designed and built; till 1956 they were built entirely of granite and thereafter faced in granite though not built of it. The granite row we occupied in that year was reputed to be amongst the last of its kind in the city. (One problem with granite, however, was its low background radiation, and this was at one time suspected as being a possible cause of the city's high leukaemia rates.) The granite gave the scheme a homogeneous and pleasing physical appearance. The houses had no central heating, being still coal- or electric-fired, and there was admittedly a minor problem of damp from the metal window frames, but there were tiled interior window ledges and the wee puddles mopped up easily.

It is difficult to imagine that in the 1950s and '60s there could have been a better housing scheme in Aberdeen, or even Scotland and possibly beyond, than Kincorth. The council tenants were carefully chosen and most of the people were skilled workers, tradesmen or routine white collar workers. I had friends in other housing estates – Northfield and Mastrick – and I was aware that the *Kinkers* was a cut or two above them in both physical and human terms. Folk from the smaller Garthdee estate across the river from Kincorth might claim an equality with us, but ours was a big scheme, about 8,000 people in the '60s, not just a *wee pucklie hooses*. Aberdeen Council was largely Labour-controlled after 1945 and it was an open secret that expanding Kincorth was aimed partly at making Aberdeen South, formerly a safe Conservative seat, into a marginal one – which it became after Labour won it for the first time in 1966. Although there were some floating voters around, most Kincorth folk at that time, despite having moved up in the world, were Labour supporters.

In some ways life in Kincorth for bairns was similar to that in Torry. Very few people had cars in the mid-1950s (a few, like my father, had a works van, and there was a salesman across the street with a car) so we still played in the street and it was still the same pastimes. As well as – obviously – football, rounders was popular and we also played Japs and British, Sappy Sodjers, Kick the Cannie, Allevie-O and other games. Fathers still generally made *cairties*, usually from old prams' wheels, and crude sledges in the winter, rather than buying them. We had girds – old tubeless cycle wheels – and raced with them, using a stick to control them. It was not a sophisticated world we inhabited, and much of it our own parents would have recognised from theirs, but with the harsh poverty removed.

Television arrived in 1955: there was just one channel, but few people could afford a set (the unit price of a TV is about the same today as it was 50 years ago); and many could not even initially afford to rent them. I was lucky, my father was by that time a radio and TV engineer, and for a while we borrowed a telly every night from the shop, not owning one. We kids didn't stay in a lot evenings, but were '*oot*'. The usual inter-generational exchange consisted of little more than:

'*Far ye gyan?*' '*Oot.*' '*Oot far?*' '*Jist oot.*'

We had lost the wonderful Torry coastline, alas, by moving to Kincorth, but had gained instead the River Dee where at the *Shakkin Briggie* we went with our bikes and swam, and also the Den of Leggat, a wonderful sunken wood round a wee loch on a Dee tributary, was added to our frontier lands. And we still had the Gramps (*The Grumps*), the range of mini-mountains Kincorth shared with Torry. Even in winter we were *oot*. We had lost the magical Torry experience of the *leerie* man coming round nightly to light the gas lamps, following him along the street and cheering when they went on. But we had electric light now – and streets empty of traffic.

I would not idealise our youthful pursuits. Some were seriously anti-social, like smashing the street lamps and the windows in the telephone boxes, or staring fires in *The Grumps*, or putting *squeebs* in empty milk bottles before ringing door bells and running away. And there were fights, bare knuckle fights that drew blood, and battles between groups of *loons* with sticks, however these conflicts assumed a ritualised character, with no-one ever really getting hurt. But there were no serious weapons. In all my days in Kincorth I never saw a knife, an axe, or even a bicycle chain used as a weapon, still less anything like a firearm. *We hid nae need o yon Frunkie Vaughan in the Kinkers. It wisnae Easterhoose.*

Actually the streets were in some ways more fun in Kincorth than in Torry. This was because, like many such schemes, there were few shops there. There were some, the Copey on Provost Watt Drive and a couple of others, but unlike Torry, most stuff came round in vans. So you had the ice cream van at night, and even occasional horse and cart traders, with whom (as well as patting and feeding the horse) you could exchange rags or scrap metal for the rubbish they gave out in return, and sometimes get a *hurlie on the cairtie* as well. We had lost the Sally Anne, but there was the Boys' Brigade, till Murdoch and I, local bad boys, were expelled from it, a real affront to my mother's respectability.

The BB was held in the local kirk. There was no pub in Kincorth, but there was a kirk; one for 8,000 people. Even allowing for the fact that some would have stayed with their auld kirks elsewhere, this is a good indication of the status of religion in the Aberdeen working class at that time. My parents were occasional kirk attenders, but few others were.

There were two primary schools. Mine had a male head and male deputy head, and a dozen or so female teachers; such were things gender-wise in the 1950s. There was no secondary school at that time (one was later built), but other things were lacking too. There was no unemployment, apart from one or two socially stigmatised characters that were assumed to be idle by choice. There were almost no unmarried mothers (or at least not visibly so, though often someone might find later in life that their big sister was actually their mother). There was no drug abuse and surprisingly little alcohol abuse either – alcohol consumption at this time was at its historical low and few people drank or even had drink in the house. The odd exception, like the stonemason across the road who staggered uphill singing from the Brig o' Dee Bar after 10pm was just that, the exception. So too was Hogmanay when for several days people would visit neighbours and relatives in an alcohol-fuelled festival. Without being romantic, in pre-TV days people actually did play banjos, spoons, and accordions and sing songs at Hogmanay. And you took coal and black bun First Fittin, and said '*Lang may yer lum reek.*'

Another thing missing was any political radicalism, or even political activity. Without exaggerating the inter-war years, there was a leaven of radical workers around in Aberdeen then. In Kincorth in the 1960s – despite, or maybe because of the still dominant Labourism – the politics of aspiration replaced those of social engagement. From the later '50s onwards, but especially from the early '60s with rising wages and the increasing array of consumer commodities available, living standards began to markedly improve from the austerity of the '40s and mid-'50s. I left the Kinkers in 1969 and by then everyone had a TV. Fewer had fridges, washing machines or telephones, but some did and the others aspired to them, as did most people to the car that was still, though ownership was increasing, just beyond the reach of the majority. Aspiration took other forms too. A *lumper* (fish market porter) across the road caused a local sensation when he gave up his job and trained to be a school teacher once mature student grants became available, but the main channel of aspiration was for the children. Out of my primary class of about 30, around a dozen, including myself, went to senior secondary schools in the city centre after passing the 11-plus exam. Several of us went on to university.

The British Labour movement and the British working class were always given over to what used to be called 'gas-and-water socialism'. Not for them the high theoretical concerns of the German working class movement or the militancy of the French workers, for example. Decent housing, decent educational opportunities and decent health care, within or without the capitalist system – that's what they wanted. And in Kincorth in the 1950s and '60s you could well have believed that they'd achieved it, that they had built the City on the (Kincorth) Hill, the New Jerusalem. Compared to today's majority (leaving aside the present underclass, non-existent in Kincorth then), folk back in those days had far fewer consumer goods, but full employment, decent housing, free health care, free educational opportunities. I went to the former German Democratic Republic (GDR) in the 1980s several times, by which time Western capitalism was awash with consumer affluence. The GDR was like being back in Kincorth a quarter of a century before; austerity in the sphere of consumer goods, but with the basic needs of housing, health, education and employment met. The GDR also had that overwhelming sense of respectability and cleanliness that I recall from Kincorth in the 1950s. Many people felt nostalgia (*Ostalgie*) for the GDR when it collapsed. I must be unique in having felt nostalgia there when it was still in existence – but for Kincorth. By that time the place I had known had gone. That post-war social democratic semi-collectivist, but at the same time aspirational, vision of the future which Kincorth initially represented was finally buried in the 1980s. It was replaced by (obviously to varying degrees amongst varying sections of its inhabitants) the Thatcherite vision of working class home ownership and the acquisition of shares in the privatised utilities and other industries.

You see things clearer in reverse, or as Kierkegaard said, 'We live life forwards and understand it backwards.' I had no idea till I started writing this book that my life conformed to a pattern, one of the dominant patterns of North East life. I had two grandparents from fishing backgrounds who moved into Aberdeen because of the attraction of the trawling industry and two who moved from rural Aberdeenshire into the city because of the better job prospects that were available there. This is not untypical. Both my parents were brought up in the 1920s and '30s in respectable poverty, and then left school, my mother at 14 and my father at 13 and a half, to work in textiles and as a delivery boy respectively. The War, in which my father – again typically – fought in the Gordon Highlanders and survived El Alamein, the invasion of Sicily and D-Day, transformed his life and he was trained as a radio mechanic after being wounded. In the post-war years this allowed him to work as a radio and later TV engineer and to embody the aspirant spirit of the times, in due course setting up in self-employment, buying a house before most people from his background did (he was 50 then), and encouraging his two children to go to University. Both of us, like many educated others at that time, left the town. My sister naturally went because there were few opportunities for Slavonic language librarians in Aberdeen; I left because I wanted to see the wider world beyond the Brig o' Dee. Maybe it was all that Jean-Paul Sartre I was reading, about re-creating myself on the *tabula rasa*, the slate wiped clean, of existence. Existentialism and Exile? (*The loon's gettin afa metaphorical, is he nae? It's jist the Kinkers aifter aa.*)

I would not advocate a walk around Kincorth – *It's nithing bit hooses* – but instead take the bus through the scheme to Kincorth Hill Nature Reserve (*the posh name they hiv noo for The Grumps*). Here you can get a fine overview of Kincorth and much of the city as a whole. The local council has produced a leaflet on Kincorth Hill, which gives details of its attractions and transport to the reserve (www.aberdeencity.gov.uk). As you bus through the scheme you notice the former pleasing homogeneity has gone. We were not even allowed to paint our doors a different colour from *Cooncil* regulations, but now many of the houses (snapped up in the Thatcherite right-to-buy stampede) are adorned with B&Q doors, and have extensions of varying kinds and indifferent aesthetic quality. Whatever modern Kincorth represents, it is something different from what it represented 50 years ago. But as I write this we are in the midst of the biggest economic crisis for 75 years, one that will get worse and will lead to negative equity – even in Aberdeen – to unemployment, to house repossessions as unemployment rises, to the slashing of social expenditure, to tax rises and all the rest of it.

There were a few dissenters to the optimistic consensus back in the 1950s and '60s in Kincorth. One lived across the road from me and I got to know him. He was regarded as a 'minker' because he didn't work and he took a wee drinkie. (OK, that's *two* folk in the Kinkers with an alcohol problem). He told me he couldn't work because of wounds he had got as a volunteer in Spain in the International Brigades and that – he was an old Stalinist – he was blacklisted anyway. In the apathetic times of the mid-1960s, recalling his years of political action 30 years before, he bewailed the passivity of the working class, whom he regarded as having sold their souls for a mess of consumer pottage. But he predicted these years of affluence would not last for ever, and like a fiery Old Testament Evangel he anticipated with grim satisfaction the coming retribution.

'*They'll get fit's comin tae them, they'll get fit's comin,*' he would say. It took a long time, including the Cargo Cult Capitalism of the '80s and '90s when the bulk of the population appeared to believe that there was no limit to their credit-funded material aspirations, but every prediction comes true if you wait long enough. Maybe the time of his has arrived.

Onywyse, I noo see there wis mair tae Kincorth nor hooses. And there still is. After representing the '50s social democratic consensus and then the '80s Thatcherite dream, it now stands on the verge of a new representational incarnation, as the reality of the capitalist economic cycle comes full circle. Could Kincorth become a new Torry, a once prosperous area that has seen better days? My mother was very proud of having moved from Torry to Kincorth rather than to any of the other housing schemes, and I can almost hear her from beyond the grave as I write this saying, *Aye, weel, as lang as its nae Mastrick.*

PEOPLE

CHAPTER EIGHT

Willie Thom: The Weaver Bard of Bon Accord

POSSIBLY THE MOST FAMOUS quotation in Scottish, indeed British, 19th century social history is that of Willie Thom, speaking of the condition of the handloom weavers in the early decades of the century before last. Looking back to that epoch, from the penury he and his fellows had collapsed into in the 1840s, Thom stated, in his *Rhymes and Recollections of a Handloom Weaver*:

> This was the daisy portion of weaving, the bright and midday period of all who pitched a shuttle... Four days did the weaver work, and such a week to a skilful workman brought forty shillings. Sunday, Monday and Tuesday, were of course jubilee. Lawn frills gorged freely from under the wrists of his fine, blue, gilt-buttoned coat. He dusted his head with white flour on Sunday, smirked, and wore a cane. Walked in clean slippers on Monday-Tuesday saw him talk war bravado, quote Volney and get drunk. Weaving commenced gradually on Wednesday.[1]

I have known this quotation for over 30 years, yet only recently did I discover that Thom was from my native Aberdeen and that he was a poet to boot. Indeed, in his day Thom was seen by some as 'the new Burns' and he had a meteoric rise to fame and fortune, followed sadly by an equally swift decline into renewed poverty and obscurity. While other weaver poets such as Robert Tannahill of Paisley are still remembered and their works known, who today could name a poem of Thom's or quote as much as a line of his verse?

I am not out to claim that Thom is a neglected poetic genius, but he does deserve to be remembered for more than a quotation that has almost become a cliché, and the tale of his life, which is in many ways one more interesting than his poetic efforts, deserves retelling. Thom's *Rhymes and Recollections*, published in 1844 and mentioned above, contains some poetry of modest merit, as well as a frustratingly small amount of uniquely interesting social history. Had Thom chosen autobiography rather than poetry, he would probably be much more widely remembered today.

Thom was born in 1798 or '99 in Sinclair's Close in central Aberdeen, an overcrowded slum area by the Castlegate. His mother was a widow and her problems were compounded when Willie was run over by a carriage on the Links as a bairn and left partly crippled for life. The carriage owner, the Earl of Errol, a local laird, offered Mrs Thom five shillings as compensation, which she refused. Thom got a basic education at a dame's school (a *wifie's squeel* he called it) and at ten was apprenticed as a weaver, then a very lucrative trade. Spinning had been mechanised, but not weaving, so demand for various textiles was met by a huge increase in the number of handloom weavers. Besides, there was a war with France on and the market for cloth was insatiable. Thom served his time at a factory in The Green.

Handloom weavers who could set up on their own, working from home on the domestic system, were especially favoured, as Thom's description cited above shows. Thom could not afford to set up on his own, so in 1814 he entered the weaving factory of Gordon, Barron and Co., in Schoolhill, Aberdeen. The early industrial capitalists favoured the factory system, as it gave them control over quality, price and, most importantly, conditions of work. Later with the development of power loom weaving in the 1820s, the factory owners would gradually break the back of independent domestic weaving, but in Thom's day the textile capitalists had to make do with orphans, women, ex-convicts and paupers for factory weaving work.

In his *Recollections*, Thom describes the Schoolhill factory, where he worked for 17 years, as 'a prime nursery of vice and sorrow'. It stood on the site of the present Triple Kirks, at the north end of Belmont Street, and operated from about 1770 till roughly 1830. According to Thom it employed between 300 and 400 workers.

It is a duty, do it who may – and it shall be done – to expose the factory system of that day as it stood in our 'moral north'... During my experience of 17 years within that factory the average earnings of first rate hands, varying with the times, good and bad, were from six to nine shillings a week.

Robert Gordon's College
When he worked in the Belmont Street textile factory, Thom and workmates took their lunch breaks in the gardens here. Originally a charity endowment, Gordon's later became a boys' public (ie, private) school, *bit they let in a few tinks wi bursaries, likk mysel.*

Thom also describes the prevalence of drunkenness and sexual promiscuity amongst the workers, with many of the females slipping into prostitution. One particular grievance was what he termed a savings bank in reverse; the employers fined workers heavily for late-coming and other misdemeanors, so that often at a week's end of work, there would be no pay, or the worker might even find his or herself in debt to the employer.

Thom does not deny the lighter side of his life at this time. In their work breaks, he tells that those workers interested in literature would repair to the garden of Robert Gordon's Hospital nearby and talk of, and read, Scott and Byron – but their main fare was old Scots songs and ballads. 'Poets were indeed our Priests,' he states. The works of 'the Ettrick Shepherd' (Hogg) were favoured, as were the productions of 'our ill-fated fellow craftsman, Robert Tannahill, who had just then taken himself from a neglecting world' (Tannahill committed suicide). Of course another favourite was Burns, of whom Thom stated, 'Let only break forth the healthy and vigorous chorus, "A man's a man for a' that", the fagged weaver brightens up. His very shuttle skytes boldly along, and clatters through in faithful time to the tune of his merrier shopmates.'

As a reasonable singer and an accomplished German flute player,

Thom was ever at the centre of the weavers' conviviality, acquiring a lifelong addiction to alcohol, however much he might point out the ill effects of indulgence. It was the occasion of one of these festivities that saw the birth of Thom's first published poem, in around 1826, which he sent to the *Aberdeen Journal*. Thom states that at the time he was so poor he could not afford a copy of the paper and had to ask another purchaser for confirmation that his work had indeed been printed. One account states that Thom had written the poem while in prison for taking part in a meal-mob riot, which might explain his destitution at that time. By this time weaving had, in Thom's words, become 'a waste of life, a mere permission to breathe', and the Schoolhill factory closed down in 1830. With a newly acquired wife, Thom left his home in Spa Street, near Schoolhill, and headed south the next year, to try his luck in Dundee.

Thom's Dundee years are little covered in his *Recollections*, though it appears his wife didn't settle and left him to return to Aberdeen. By 1837 he had been awhile in Newtyle, Forfarshire, working at his trade, until a great depression threw him out of work. There he had acquired a companion, Jean Whitecross, who bore him four children. For a couple of years Thom appears to have suffered great hardship, having to sell his books and even resorting to playing his flute in the streets. (The flute is currently in Aberdeen University Museum.) By 1839 Thom was back in Aberdeen, again working in a weaving factory. When the chance of domestic weaving came up, he shifted to Inverurie in 1840, renting a garret at 23 North Street, which is now demolished. It was here, from the seeming depths of despair, that Thom's fortunes were to experience their sudden, albeit brief, rise.

Thom may be largely forgotten elsewhere, but I was pleased to find that he was still 'world famous in Inverurie'. In the Carnegie Library can be found his chair and a pair of portraits of Thom, and the local Gordon District Council has produced an excellent wee pamphlet on the poet's residence in Inverurie, accompanied by a Thom Town Trail, taking you to the sites of his former house, workshop and the graveyard where his two common-law companions lie in unmarked graves.

Thom responded to the delights of the Garioch (pronounced

Geeree), the Aberdeenshire countryside around Inverurie. He would appear to have written many of the poems eventually published under his name whilst at Inverurie; hence he is often (somewhat inaccurately) titled The Inverurie Poet. His conviviality had not deserted him, and he still played his flute socially and was a member of a local band which performed commercially in the Garioch. He also enjoyed the freedom of domestic weaving while it lasted, but it ended and he was soon out of work again. In addition, his companion Jean died and he and his children faced the coming winter without means of support. Contemplating a move back to Aberdeen to throw himself upon the parish and enter the poorhouse, in despair Thom sent off one of his poetic creations to the *Aberdeen Herald*, announcing it as the product of 'a Serf, who has to weave fourteen hours of the four and twenty'. The poem, *The Blind Boy's Pranks*, was published on 2 January 1841 and Thom became a sensation.

The poem was reproduced in many other publications, including the *Aberdeen Journal*, where it was read by the landowner Gordon of Knockespock. He was impressed and sent Thom £5 through the newspaper's editor. There followed a letter from Knockespock asking the weaver-poet for details of himself, apparently with the view to finding Thom a teaching post where he could abandon his industrial serfdom and give over more time to his poetic talents. Thom replied with a disingenuous piece of spin in the form of a CV which pressed all the right buttons, assuring Gordon of Knockespock that he was a devout Christian, mentioning the deceased Jean as his 'wife' rather than as his companion. With a fair degree of inaccuracy Thom described himself as a moderate drinker, stating, 'I don't drink, as little at any rate as possible.' Within three months Thom was in London at Gordon's invitation, being lionised by polite society.

The period 1841–44 was the 'daisy portion' of Thom's brief life. On his return from three months in London he was fêted at a dinner in the Royal Hotel by 50 gentlemen, the cream of Aberdeen society. His poems began to appear regularly in the *Aberdeen Herald* and were published in volume form in 1844 to great critical acclaim and financial success. The volume was tactfully dedicated to Mrs Gordon, the wife of his patron. Thom had money to burn and spent much of it in conviviality with his poetic cronies in the howffs and clubs of Huxter Row in Aberdeen. The temptation of a salary of £50 a year to work for the publishers Chambers in Edinburgh was one he could easily turn down in his new financial state, though in retrospect such work might have been his salvation. Indeed, he set up as a weaving capitalist himself, putting out work to other weavers and employing an agent to manage the business. 'If you want to help me, buy my webs,' he told those who tried to encourage him to more genteel employment. Thom preferred the tavern.

Thom was persuaded by Gordon to take up residence in London late in 1844. His three-year stay was to prove his downfall. The idea was to produce a second edition of his poems, which was done, but it was a financial failure. In London the weaver's poetic muse all but dried up and he produced little work of note. However admirers supplied the want and also supplied the money – for a while. A list of sub-scribers in Calcutta sent Thom £300, whilst another in America gave him £400. He was entertained in high society in the studio of the painter Chantrey and in the salon of Lady Blessington. Thom also met Dickens several times and must have told him the story of his own crippling as a child. In Dickens' *Tale of Two Cities*, there occurs the story of a child invalided by a nobleman's carriage, whose father throws back into the carriage the meagre compensation offered. One rich admirer, John Mouat, even took Thom on a trip to Paris, where the poet got lost and was later found by his patron asking every French passer-by, '*Is there nae man in this big toun, that can tell a puir body the wye haim?*'

Thom kept open house at his residence at 40 Charlotte Terrace in London, giving help to impecunious poets and hosting visits from equally impecunious Chartists, ie those involved in the struggle for the Charter, whose Six Points included giving working men the vote. He also, in the disapproving words of one writer, 'procured a new consort from Inverurie, by whom he had several children'. She was called Jean Stephen. Thom continued to drink and live the bohemian life, and by the end of 1847 was effectively bankrupt.

'The siller had run through my hands like a pickle dry sand,' he later commented. To escape his threatening creditors, he left London and came back to Scotland, but not to Aberdeen. Possibly not wanting to return in disgrace to the city where he had so recently been celebrated, Thom settled in Dundee, at Hawkhill. Poor, neglected and very ill, he died on 29 February 1848, and had a well-attended public funeral. A monument was raised over his grave in the Western Cemetery in the city in 1857.

In the century and a half since his death, Thom has largely been forgotten.

The Weaver-Poet
A fine portrait of the bard at the height of his fame, from his *Rhymes and Recollections of a Handloom Weaver.* His fall would be swift as he took to alcohol and his rich patrons abandoned him.

His poems for the most part are fairly conventional productions in the Scots language, often thickly overlaid with Victorian sentimentality, as in *The Overgate Orphan*:

> Ye creep to a breast, Jamie, cauld as the snaw
> Ye hang roun' a heart Jamie, sinkin awa
> I'm laith, laith to leave ye, though fain would I dee
> Gin Heaven would lat my lost laddie wi' me!

Thom's most interesting poem, and his longest, is *Whisperings for the Unwashed,* and in it his social and political opinions are forcefully expressed. In the oft-quoted paragraph from the *Recollections,* Thom mentions Volney as one of his influences. Volney was a radical writer of the French Revolution with a vision of the ultimate triumph of rationality and science and the banishing or ignorance and want, and he influenced many early 19th century radicals. Certainly Thom thought the country in need of reform and wrote to a friend about his visit to the House of Commons to listen to the debates in 1841:

> Their doings and manners would disgrace a common tap room, and in manner and in result God knows how well the groaning millions of our day can tell.

Elsewhere he stated further, 'I have listened to the eloquence and heard the nonsense of those who would give laws to the people.'

Most of Thom's Victorian commentators state that, beyond some sympathy with Chartist aims, he had no interest in politics. But a long out-of-print book by Robert Bruce, *Willie Thom: The Inverurie Poet, a New Look* (1970), shows that this view is quite wrong. Bruce's grandfather knew Thom in Inverurie, where in the early 1840s the pair produced a short-lived radical publication, *The Gossamer*, which was forced to close because of local hostility. Thom mixed with Chartists like Julian Harney in London and sympathised with their views about extending voting rights to working men. He spoke at Chartist meetings in the capital and at one Bruce quotes him as saying:

> I know the working-man's associations, know the national association and its tendencies. I am proud to own my friendship with its daring purpose, the creation of a broad bannock and a short parliament.

Harney, who was later to first publish Marx's *Communist Manifesto* in English, was a great friend of Thom's, and they corresponded and visited each other's houses. Another regular visitor at the Harney's, whom Thom may well have met, was Friedrich Engels, later Marx's close collaborator. Thom wrote for Harney's Chartist newspaper, *The Northern Star*. In a letter in possession of Bruce's grandfather, Harney states that he kept Thom's name out of the paper on one occasion, as he feared that publicising his Chartist connections would upset the poet's literary supporters and patrons. Long after he had been abandoned by others, Thom cited Harney's friendship as something which sustained him. He was also a close friend of WJ Fox, one of the leaders of the Anti-Corn Law League, and the poet wove a banner as a table cover for the League. So much for the non-political Thom!

Agitation for the Charter and the abolition of the Corn Laws, which kept the price of bread artificially high, were at their height when *Whisperings for the Unwashed* was written and they clearly underlie its narrative. The poem starts with a depiction of the thoughtless, sleeping rich, '*saft the pillow to the fat man's pow*', and is especially critical of the landed interest (a footnote to the poem criticises the Corn Laws explicitly):

> An' cozie the happin o the farmer's bed
> The feast o yestreen how it oozes through
> In bell and blab on his burly brow

Meanwhile the weavers are woken up by the town's drummer:

> Rubadub, rubadub, row-row-row
> Hark, how he waukens the Weavers now!

Their miserable condition is described:

> Wi hungry wame and hopeless breast
> Their food no feeding, their sleep no rest.
> Arouse ye, ye sunken, unravel your rags
> No coin in your coffers, no meal in your bags.

The Chartists were divided between physical and moral force wings. Whilst 'the physicals' believed violence was justified in order to gain the vote for working men, the moral force wing eschewed it. Thom clearly sympathised with the latter viewpoint, as shown when he insists:

> Arouse ye, but neither with bludgeon nor blow
> Let mind be your armour, darkness your foe.

And he ends the poem with a series of references that are pure Volney, with a vision of a rational future:

> When fair Science gleams over city and plain
> When Truth walks abroad all unfetter'd again...

The poem's last words sum up Thom's humanistic yearnings:

MAN LONGS FOR HIS RIGHT.

He was no Burns. But Willie Thom deserves to be remembered for more than a single famous paragraph of prose.

Note

[1] *Rhymes and Recollections of a Handloom Weaver*, first published in 1844, was re-issued in 1880 with an extended Preface, 'The Life of William Thom' by W Skinner.

CHAPTER NINE

Proletarian Pilgrimage:
A Forgotten Classic

AUTOBIOGRAPHIES BY WORKING CLASS people are quite rare, especially ones from the pens of those who remained manual workers for much of their lives. The paucity of proletarian memoirs makes it all the more frustrating that one which does exist and describes working class labour and social life, as well as including accounts of important political events and personages, has been out of print for over 70 years. This is a book by John Paton entitled *Proletarian Pilgrimage*, which was published in 1935 and dedicated to his friend and fellow North East of Scotland socialist, no less a person than Lewis Grassic Gibbon.

Paton's book is notable for more than its dedication to Scotland's greatest 20th century novelist. This memoir covers his involvement in socialist politics from the time of the Boer War to the aftermath of World War One. It also gives an account of Paton's working life, both in Aberdeen and later in Glasgow, from his time as a printer's apprentice, through his employment in a variety of other trades and occupations, until he eventually became the proprietor of his own hairdresser's shop. The book additionally has observations on the politics and personalities of key Independent Labour Party figures, from Ramsay MacDonald and Keir Hardie to James Maxton. By the time he wrote *Proletarian Pilgrimage* Paton had been working full time for the ILP for a decade and a half, and was a major figure in that grouping at the time of its maximum influence, being at various times both its general secretary and the editor of its paper, *New Leader,* through the 1920s and early '30s.

Paton awaits his biographer. He has finally made the pages of the latest, 2004, edition of the *Dictionary of National Biography*, where the author of his entry, David Howell, outlines the main events of his life. But as far as *Proletarian Pilgrimage* goes, it is possibly dismissed too readily as a volume of 'whimsical' autobiography. Accounts of the Scottish Labour movement in the 20th century seldom mention Paton at all, and his book even less. In my view the work is a very useful and neglected source for working class history. And beyond that it is simply a great read, full of interest and humour.

Paton was born in 1886 in Aberdeen, which he describes as 'a town of many smallish industries, [its] provincialism bred of isolation and self sufficiency'. Certainly in terms of its labour force Aberdeen was self sufficient, for the industrial growth and the quadrupling in size of the city in the 19th century had found its workers almost entirely recruited from its own rural hinterland. His own family is a paradigm of this situation, from his grandmother, a former rural domestic servant, to his father, a country baker who came to Aberdeen to set up his own business. This failed, and when he was subsequently suspected of arson for insurance purposes, his father fled whilst Paton was a baby.

What is interesting about these and Paton's other family members is that most of them struggled unsuccessfully to attain petty bourgeois status in the new urban world. His grandmother possessed a tiny grocer's shop and lorded it over the local lumpen proletariat, granting them tick with scorn from her seat in the shop, which the locals called 'The Throne'. 'Brucie', as she was known, despite having fled to Aberdeen to 'cover her shame' at falling pregnant, epitomised the Victorian struggle for respectability of many working class people. When her daughter married a coal heaver, 'Brucie' shut herself in a room and refused to speak to her daughter right up to her death. The struggle for respectability at this time, which covered a deep hypocrisy, is well covered in many incidents in Paton's childhood narrative, as too are the sordid realities of the pawnshop, the *menoge* (primitive mutual credit), the annual house flitting and working class marriage rituals.

Leaving school at 13, Paton was initiated into the world of work as a printer's apprentice with *The Aberdeen Free Press*. Interestingly he describes this as a 'genteel' occupation, stating, 'The apprentices were all considerably older than me and only one or two were from working class families. A seven-year apprenticeship was a formidable [financial] obstacle to the average working class parent.'

For two years Paton was a copy boy, running errands for the journalists, which he hugely enjoyed, but at 15 he started to work at the machines. Paton had no appetite for industrial discipline: 'Typesetting, which I'd found so full of interest, had lost the charm of novelty. The long years which stretched ahead of me looked dreary and extremely unattractive.' As was often to happen in his working life, Paton got himself constructively dismissed, on this occasion by kicking a foreman.

He was next apprenticed as a baker, which he liked better than the genteel world of *The Aberdeen Free Press*, not least since there he was initiated into the mysteries of sex by the female workers. Of the bakery he notes (this was in 1901), 'Politics and sport had not yet become major interests. Bakehouse gossip was soon exhausted. But there was one topic which seemed inexhaustible – women and sex generally.'

He also talks about his own efforts to interest females by Walking the Carpet, as he puts it, with fellow youths. This consisted of pounding the Union Street pavements engaging in sexual badinage. Now, *wakkin the mat* as it was subsequently known, continued in full force in Aberdeen till World War Two, but at what point did the carpet become a more plebian mat?

The baker's job lasted only a year; soon Paton found a job that lacked the discipline of productive labour, becoming a barber. The reason for this change, he says, was an injury which made him limp and he was therefore unsuited for the long standing entailed in baking, though barbers stood as much, if not more than, bakers. Paton liked variety and interest and – for a while – he found it working in a barber's shop in the East End of Aberdeen. Some of his descriptions of the job are awesome, as when for example trawlermen, home from two weeks at sea, were shaven:

> Antiseptics were unknown. The customer was lathered with a brush already plentifully filled with soap from the previous customer, much smeared with coal dust and speckled with herring-scales. (There was) no extra charge for removing a

fortnight's stubble, sometimes glued together with an amalgam of fish-scales, sweat and sea salt. Sometimes the job was complicated by the fisherman having a speckled necklet of salt water boils circling his throat.

Paton had already become a reader when he broke his leg and was confined to bed for a while as a boy. But the reading of this 10 year old, working his way through Dickens and Scott as well as Motley's *The Rise of the Dutch Republic* and Mommsen's *History of Rome*, is astonishing today. Even given the 19th century tradition of the working class autodidact, this is prodigious. Paton's fellow barbers introduced him to socialism via *The Clarion*, and he was soon taking part in the outings of the Clarion Scouts. In one they deliberately disrupted the King's visit to Aberdeen to open the new Marisichal College by clanking noisily past the ceremony with their picnic equipment. Paton broadened his reading: Blatchford, Haekel, Huxley and others were devoured, and he was soon a member of the fledgling local branch of the ILP.

One interesting omission from Paton's reading list was Marx. Despite his early rejection of religion, Paton remained basically an ethical socialist, with a fairly weak theoretical underpinning. In this regard the broad church of the ILP was ideal for him. Its main rival in Aberdeen at this time was the Marxist Social Democratic Federation, and Paton describes the rivalry between these two at public meetings in Aberdeen's Castlegate

ABERDEEN CORPORATION
PUBLIC HEALTH DEPARTMENT
PREVENTION OF CONSUMPTION
You are earnestly requested to abstain from the dangerous and objectionable habit of SPITTING

Health Warning
Before the First World War public health in Aberdeen's overcrowded pre-industrial slums was on some indexes worse than Glasgow's levels. Tuberculosis was widespread when Paton was an ILP stalwart.

stance at the time. Though also small, the SDF was a more significant force in the city than the ILP, and had almost created a spectacular first when in 1896 its candidate, Tom Mann, backed by the Aberdeen Trades Council, had come within 500 votes of ousting the Liberal MP for Aberdeen North.

But swapping insults with the SDF at the Castlegate was not enough for Paton. On leaving his printer's job he had said he wanted 'freedom, excitement, constant change and variety', things which were not readily available in provincial Aberdeen in the 1900s. A friend had gone to Glasgow and 'His talk revealed a new freedom in an altogether more exciting and wider world. Aberdeen visibly shrank in his presence. I began to long for experience of this braver and more colourful life. [I decided] to try my luck in Glasgow.' So, after getting himself sacked again, Paton's pilgrimage took him to the Second City of the Empire, which was not to disappoint him.

Glasgow certainly provided Paton with an excitement lacking in Aberdeen. As well as taking trips *'doon the watter'* he discovered Glasgow gang life in an encounter with the 'Coliseum Boys' of the Gorbals, and attended an early Old Firm match on Ne'er day at Parkhead, which both appalled and fascinated him:

> The match had less the spirit of a sporting event than of a gladiatorial contest. The rivals in the arena clashed in a frenzy of zeal; their scores of thousands of partisans bellowed with rage, hurling wild insults at each other. The affair ended in dozens of free fights between the fanatic supporters of the teams.

In Glasgow Paton fell passionately in love with a beautiful Jewess, hardly an option in mono-cultural Aberdeen, but was shown the door by her father (who ran a tailoring sweatshop based on illegal Jewish immigrant labour) when he discovered that Paton was an atheist. Paton found the Glasgow women feisty and eventually married one. But he made the interesting observation that his wife had no domestic skills, adding, 'In this she was typical. It was the exception for a working girl in Glasgow to have the taste for, or proficiency in, housewifery.' Again this was so unlike Aberdeen, where domesticity was the aim, and women who married almost universally gave up work as a mark of 'respectability'.

1906 was an exciting year to arrive in Glasgow. The LRC (Labour Representation Committee) had just won 29 seats in Parliament and was soon to form the Labour Party. Options for political activity were so much greater than they had been in Aberdeen. Paton worked an 80-hour week in a barbers shop in Cowcaddens and was sacked for trying to enlist his fellow workers in a union, then blacklisted for a while at his trade. Interestingly, this is virtually the only time in a biography spanning 30 years that Paton mentions industrial struggle. For the ILP politics meant elections, and neither in Aberdeen or Glasgow did any of the branches he joined appear to devote any time at all to the huge industrial struggles that characterised the first two decades of the 20th century. Paton travelled as far as Montrose to support the ILP in a by-election (and met Keir Hardie and Jim Larkin in the campaign), but did not engage in any activity relating to local industrial conflict on Clydeside. He makes no mention of strikes such as that at Singer's in Clydebank in 1911, or of the existence of industrially based organisations like the Socialist Labour Party (SLP). He also never mentions John Maclean, which is surprising considering that Maclean was already a prominent figure in Glasgow during Paton's residency.

The Bridgeton ILP, astonishingly since John Maxton won it for the party in 1922 with over 60 per cent of the vote, had a mere 20 members at this time and indulged largely in open-air meetings at Brigton Cross. In Partick the party organised free speech demonstrations, and Paton gives an interesting account of how they were attacked and routed in Dumbarton Road by the local Orangemen:

> We'd proceeded a few hundred yards when, from both sides and from a dozen points, compact bodies of Orangemen erupted from the side streets and charged through us. We found our-selves in a sea of fierce faces and whirling fists.
>
> We'd no chance at all against them. They were all tough fellows from the shipyards who enjoyed nothing so much as

the opportunity for a good fight. It wasn't a defeat, it was a rout. We fled in all directions.

But the defeat rankled and for a time groups of us sedulously practiced walking stick drill under an ex-army instructor. Fortunately the trouble died away mysteriously before we were called upon to exhibit our skill.

He eventually got another hairdresser's job in Springburn. There, the ILP branch was quite strong and composed almost entirely of working men, mainly skilled trade unionists. Many of them were Catholics, which possibly causes us to question how far, in reality, Catholics were debarred from skilled trades at that time; in Springburn, with its railway shops, apparently they were not. But the ever-restless Paton fell out with his Springburn comrades when he took up the case of Fransciso Ferrer, the Spanish anarchist executed by the clerical regime in Catholic Spain. In an anti-clerical coup, he and his associates took over the Springburn ILP and most of the Catholic workers left. A counter coup later put him out of the branch – and out of his job in the area.

He was able to acquire work in a dental business, in the days of pre-NHS quackery. Without training he was sent out to perform extractions and sell dental fittings in Glasgow and the surrounding areas; at least, unlike his fellow employees, Paton stayed sober at this work. Paton was not successful at this job, and finally gave it up after a trip to a mining village, where the men were on short time. The women invited him in for a dish of tea and listened to his sales talk, before one replied,

Eh, laddie, its nae teeth we want, but something tae eat wi' the teeth we hae!

He drifted from job to job, with periods of unemployment given over to studying in the Mitchell Library and in correspondence courses with Ruskin College. It was at this time that Paton first read Marx, though that writer appears not to have made any greater impact on him that any of the other wide variety of political authors he devoured. Soon

Paton's political life was given an unexpected new direction by attending an anarchist meeting. His recent experiences in the ILP had made him ripe for this development and for a time he was very active in the Glasgow anarchist group, headed by the Englishman George Barrett. It was quite an exciting time to be an anarchist, as in the aftermath of the Siege of Sydney Street and the affair of Peter the Painter, the term was on everyone's lips, and the Glasgow group suffered police harassment and attempted penetration.

At this time Paton was working as a milk delivery man and he describes the methods of adulteration and short measures that were practiced by the industry at that time, as well as the appalling hygiene standards in his particular dairy establishment. The travelling this work involved also allowed him to observe interesting aspects of working class life in Glasgow, including what he called his 'communist colony', a group of unskilled labourers in a slum to whom he delivered milk:

> The men were dockers with very irregular work. Both men and women drank heavily when they had the means. They were much given to rowing amongst themselves but always ready to combine against the stranger. They'd a clan spirit which ensured a constant helpfulness in their mutual relations.
>
> They developed a system of sharing which I watched with interest. Mrs Smith's man had worked yesterday and therefore she was in funds today. Mrs Thomson's man had not worked for several days but was getting a job tomorrow. Mrs Smith lent Mrs Thomson supplies for today and tomorrow in the sure knowledge that in the days after, when she was short, Mrs Thomson would provide for her. It was a regular system... a form of primitive communism.

Paton quite suddenly decided (the date is unclear, but it was some time before 1914) to return to Aberdeen. The doctor had advised him to avoid the walking associated with his milk round and he returned to his former barber's trade in his home town. Incidentally, for reasons not explained, at this time he broke with the anarchists and re-joined the ILP. Possibly the experience of police harassment had chastened him. It is clear from reading his book that Paton was not the stuff of which heroes or martyrs were made.

The socialist movement in Aberdeen had made some advances in Paton's absence, but initially he took little part in it, again for reasons not fully explained. Nor when war broke out did he do any more than make the token gesture of refusing to support the carnage. Instead, in these years Paton was steadily building up a lucrative business for himself as a hairdresser in Aberdeen with his own high-class clientele. The proletarian pilgrim was in serious danger of becoming a petty bourgeois one. His inactivity mirrored that of the ILP. With no perspective in their political armoury of anti-militarism or industrial agitation against the war, the ILP's response to the imperialist carnage was one of inertia. Paton himself says:

> But at these times, always came the difficulty: what could one do... I'd a curious sense of detachment from the terrific upheaval all around me.

This was not a dilemma other anti-war activists, such as John Maclean, encountered. Eventually the Aberdeen ILP branch, and Paton, were rescued from three years of virtual inactivity – by an election, the only form of political activity with which they were comfortable.

A by-election took place in Aberdeen South and the Union for Democratic Control put up an anti-war candidate supported by the ILP. Ramsay MacDonald came to speak to a meeting at the Music Hall, but most of the 3,000 audience were hostile and he was unable to make his speech. At a subsequent meeting some of the ILP stewards adopted an unorthodox approach to suppressing wreckers, thus allowing their speakers a hearing. One of these stewards was a character called Fraser Mac who had been a professional pugilist before becoming a socialist. An election meeting was packed with those intent on disruption and Fraser Mac invited the leader of the hecklers to come backstage and talk personally to MacDonald. The disrupter did as invited and was laid senseless by the martial arts expert, then dumped onto the meeting platform. Fraser Mac then asked the patriots, *'Dae any more o' ye*

Unemployment Relief
Apparently, without unemployment insurance, the main hope of the unemployed
before WWI was of bumping into a couple of Art Nouveau maidens in Union
Street. The one on the right might possibly drap one of her heids in your bunnet
for soup.

want to see Ramsay MacDonald?' and the meeting went peacefully.
Mac's friend Jake, another pugilist, assured that another such meeting
with a large number of hostile Gordon Highlanders behaved itself
impeccably, by knocking out the first two on-leave soldiers who
came in the meeting door with aggressive intent.

Paton had meanwhile become the local ILP secretary for the whole
of the North East and also a local town councillor in Aberdeen. The

attractions of a political career began to beckon and it looked like he might become the candidate for Aberdeen North in the 1918 election. This was the overwhelmingly working class constituency which Tom Mann had almost seized back in 1896. It was to be one of the few seats Labour won in Scotland in the Khaki Election of 1918. But Paton's anti-war stance was seen as a potential vote-loser, and the pro-war Labour jingoist Frank Rose was chosen – and elected – instead. But the growth of the ILP offered Paton another prize, that of working for the party. One feels that had this opportunity for a political career not opened up, Paton might well have remained in his comfortable salon and become the barber of the bourgeoisie.

Proletarian Pilgrimage ends with Paton becoming a full-time organiser for the ILP in 1919. The subsequent part of his life is full of interest and was partly described in the second volume of autobiography *Left Turn*, which appeared in 1936. He stood twice in Scotland as an ILP candidate, in North Ayrshire in 1922 and in his native South Aberdeen the following year, without success. He moved to London as national ILP organiser in 1924, becoming the party's general secretary in 1927 and editor of *New Leader* in 1930. He supported disaffiliation from the Labour Party in 1932, as MacDonald's economic orthodoxy was imposed as a response to the world economic crisis, but unavailingly opposed subsequent moves within the ILP to work closer with the Communist Party in a United Front policy. His youthful hostility to the Marxist SDF was carried over to its successor Marxist organisation, the Communist Party. He left the ILP in 1933, re-joining the Labour Party by 1936 and standing unsuccessfully for Norwich in 1938. After the war, he represented Norwich from 1945 until his retrial in 1964. Paton was also active in campaigning for penal reform and for the end of the death penalty, reflecting his ethical socialism. He died in 1976 at the age of 90.

John Paton was no major thinker, or even a systematic one. He was a self-educated working man whose socialism came from the heart rather than from any theoretical understanding. Neither was he much of a working class hero and it is difficult not to see self-interest at the kernel of much of his decision-making. But the book is a well-written and hugely readable account of many aspects of working class life over three decades. It also gives us glimpses of and insights into some of the main political figures in the Labour movement in those years. But what remains with me most, after several readings, are the numerous cameos of unsung working class activists like Fraser Mac, who enliven the pages of *Proletarian Pilgrimage*. It is a sad reflection on Scottish culture that this book has been so long unavailable when so much dross is regularly reprinted.

The author of this book has been attempting to persuade Luath Press to republish Paton's classic. If enough readers write in supporting the idea, it might happen.

CHAPTER TEN

The Other Name on the Everest Memorial: Alexander Kellas, Himalayan Pioneer

AT THE FOOT OF THE Rongbuk Glacier, on the north side of Mount Everest, is a memorial built in 1924 commemorating Mallory and Irvine who lost their lives on the mountain that year. The memorial also pays tribute to the Sherpas who died on the previous expedition of 1922. It finally honours a man, Alexander Kellas, who was the first to lose his life in the pursuit of climbing the highest mountain in the world. This was on a survey which took place in 1921, to prepare the way for a full assault the following year.

It is fitting that Alexander Mitchell Kellas is pulled from the obscurity into which he has sunk and recognised for what he was, the most accomplished Himalayan mountaineer of his time. Comparing Kellas with his companions of 1921 – who included Mallory himself – Walt Unsworth states in his monumental work *Everest* that 'in terms of Himalayan experience he was the greatest of all'. His obituary in the *Aberdeen Free Press* of 1921 praised the 'series of brilliant exploring and mountaineering expeditions' of local lad Kellas. So who was this man, now little known in his native North East or in Scotland? Kellas was born in 1868 into a middle class family in Aberdeen, his father being secretary to the Marine and Mercantile Board. This was the time of the great expansion of Aberdeen Harbour in response to industrial growth and prosperity. He attended the Grammar School and later Heriot-Watt College, Edinburgh and University College, London. He studied Chemistry and travelled to Heidelberg in Germany to complete his PhD. Kellas' impressive CV was enough for him to obtain a post under the Glasgow-born

William Ramsay at University College London in 1892. Ramsay was the most brilliant chemist of his day and was to receive the Nobel Prize in Chemistry in 1904 for his work on the inert gases. Also working at University College under Ramsay was Norman Collie, who was establishing his reputation both as a research chemist and as a mountaineer of international standing. In Aberdeen Kellas had already wandered the Cairgorm mountains, climbed Mount Keen in 1883 and spent several nights under the Shelter Stone below Cairn Gorm in 1887. But Collie introduced Kellas to serious mountaineering, and along with another University College worker, Morris Travers, Kellas went with Collie on a trip to the Highlands in 1895. On this trip Collie and Travers made the first ascent of Castle Ridge on Ben Nevis. Collie was a difficult man, but as with everyone who met Kellas, Collie took a great liking to him, proposing him for membership of the Scottish Mountaineering Club in 1897.

One thing the scientific pair shared in common was a 'belief' in the Grey Man of Ben MacDhui. Collie made the Grey Man famous at a Cairngorm Club dinner in 1925 when he claimed an encounter with the creature. Collie had already mentioned this encounter in New Zealand a quarter of a century before, and according to Affleck Gray in his book, *The Grey Man of Ben MacDhui*, Kellas then wrote to Collie corroborating his story by claiming a similar one with *Am Fear Liath Mor*. Gray was however clearly unaware that Collie and Kellas were friends, colleagues and climbing partners, and it is difficult not to believe that the origins of this legend lie in the corridors of University College, and the thing was a spoof between the two. Interestingly, Kellas' brother Henry, who remained in Aberdeen and practiced as a lawyer, and who was with Kellas on the supposed ghostly sighting, later remembered nothing of the affair.

While Kellas was still in Aberdeen the Cairngorm Club was founded in 1887, and it established itself as the first really viable mountaineering club in the land. Like other mountaineering clubs of the time it was composed of the urban professional and business classes, who had discovered that the great outdoors gave them a place to socialise, exercise, patriotically celebrate events such as Victoria's Jubilee and generally be 'humbled by the glory and majesty of the Creator's handiwork on earth', in the words of an early Hon. President. The foundation, but still more the survival of the Cairngorm Club from 1887 till today, with its (occasionally intermittent) production of a highly readable *Journal,* is an indication that the provincial – or parochial – cast of the local Aberdeen psyche stretched even into mountaineering.

The remit of the club was, and remained, largely within the local Cairngorm Mountains, and the continental Alps, the proving ground for mountaineers at that time, was not part of their intellectual horizon. Even the rest of Scotland remained largely a *terra incognita* for them. There is a North East ditty that might well sum up the club's philosophy:

Fecht for Britain?
Nae ava
Fecht for Scotland?
Hoots, man, na
But for Lochnagar?
By tooth and claw!

There are geographical reasons for this. From Glasgow or Edinburgh there is a radius of mountaineering possibilities to the western and central Highlands, with even the English Lakes not far away. From Aberdeen it is a logistical problem to go anywhere other than the Cairngorms. Even the Dundonians have the option of the Cairngorms plus easier access to the central Highlands than hillgoers from Aberdeen. My own mountaineering days till I left Aberdeen in 1973 were predominantly spent in the Cairngorms, generally the eastern ones, for that very reason.[1]

The club's greatest claim to fame at this time was that in 1890 it put 162 people on the summit of Mount Keen at the same time; it was a summit record then and is probably still one now. But this was not a context which bred great mountaineers. Only by moving away from Aberdeen to link up with Collie and others could Kellas broaden his horizons and contacts, and further his potential as a mountaineer. The year Kellas went with Collie to Ben Nevis, 1895, was also the

THE CAIRNGORM CLUB

First Spring Excursion.
Mount Keen,
5ᵗʰ May. 1890.

The Cairngorm Club
The context of Aberdeen mountaineering
was provided by those who came
together to form the club in 1887.
Here we have the programme
announcing the meet which resulted
in the Mount Keen mass ascent.

year of the latter's pioneering attempt, with Mummery, on Nanga Parbat, the first 8,000 metre peak ever attempted. It was fortunate for mountaineering that Kellas' scientific interests took him to London, and ultimately the Himalaya, a half century or more before Cairngorm Club members trod the Greater Ranges. From London, Kellas moved on from the Scottish mountains to Alpine climbing. He also moved on (unlike Collie), away from Ramsay to take up a job lecturing in chemistry at the Middlesex Hospital Medical School in 1896. Here he developed his interest in high-altitude physiology and started his investigations into the effects of oxygen – or the lack of it – on the human body.

At this time people were very unsure about whether human beings could live at all above about 25,000ft without oxygen; a crucial issue for any attempt on Everest, whose conquest was already being mooted in mountaineering and colonial quarters. Of this scientific research by Kellas, Collie was to state in his obituary in the *Alpine Journal* in 1921, 'he (Kellas) was probably the best authority on the subject... [of] the effects of high altitude on the human system'. Kellas' investigations were published in the *Journal of the Royal Geographical Society* of 1917 where he stated his opinion that:

A man in first-class training, acclimatized to maximum possible altitude, could make the ascent of Mount Everest without adventitious aids (ie oxygen IRM), provided the physical difficulties above 25,000ft are not prohibitive.

Despite the fact that Kellas' view would appear to be that any advantage in using oxygen would be more than counterbalanced by the weight of the apparatus itself, he took part in attempts to design and test oxygen equipment for the Everest expedition of 1921. During the war Kellas had to carry the burden of extra work at the Middlesex Hospital, covering for those on war service. This, added to the fact that he was already struggling with mental health problems, led to a collapse in his mental and physical state in 1918, which forced his early retirement. One cannot psycho-analyse the dead, but the fact that Kellas heard voices threatening violence indicates that he was possibly suffering for what we now know as paranoid schitzophrenia.

Alexander Kellas
People commented on Kellas's unkempt and uncouth appearance. He does not immediately strike you as a Himalayan mountaineer, but behind the appearance was a man of great strength and determination.

He returned to Aberdeen to recuperate and regained his health, though he was possibly fatally weakened without knowing it. In Aberdeen he gave exhibitions of his photographs to the Cairngorm Club and to the local SMC branch, including the first-ever pictures of Everest itself, purporting to show the north-east ridge which was initially thought to be the best line of assault. This image was actually taken by a Sherpa sent on for the purpose, not Kellas, and – unlike so many others at the time – he gave the Sherpa full credit for the image, never claiming it as his own. These photographs were the product of several trips Kellas had made to the Himalaya, especially to Sikkim and the Garhwal, before the war, and immediately after the conflict.

Some people then and now have thought that Kellas was the man to lead the Everest reconnaissance expedition of 1921, a venture which did not intend to climb the actual peak. By this time Kellas had had several Himalayan seasons since his first in 1907; he had more high-altitude experience than any man alive and a greater knowledge of the Himalaya than anyone. In the Sikkim Himalaya, he had made first ascents of Langpo Peak (22,800ft), Pauhunri (23,180ft) Chomiumo (22,430ft) as well as Kangchenjau (22,700ft). Further west in the Garhwal Himalaya in 1920 he attained 23,600ft on Kamet, around 2,000ft from the top, where many believe only a porters' rebellion prevented him and his companion Morshead from summiting.

Despite this encounter with the porters, Kellas was a great believer in using the locals for logistical support. Collie notes that he was popular with them and took great care of their food and comfort. Indeed before Kellas, British Himalayan expeditions used mainly Gurkhas from the Indian Army; it was Kellas who, in a remote valley, is mainly responsible for discovering the group which was to prove even better adapted to mountaineering – the Sherpas. One such, Tenzing, was subsequently with Hillary in the 1953 Everest triumph. Probably, though, in the racially charged atmosphere of the British Empire at that time, this was Kellas' undoing, for the Secretary of the Alpine Club, JP Farrar, effectively vetoed Kellas' leadership and helped put the 1921 expedition in the hands of a military man, Lieutenant Colonel Howard Bury, instead. Unsworth cites Farrar as writing (showing inaccuracy as well as prejudice):

> Kellas has never climbed a mountain, but has only walked about a steep snow slope with a lot of coolies, and the only

time they got to a very steep place they all tumbled down and ought to have been killed.

But the expedition could not do without Kellas. Indeed he was out in Sikkim already, exploring, before they arrived at Darjeeling. Kellas was among the first to note that Everest had a local name, recording the term Chha-mo-lung-ma, or Chomolunga as it is now rendered. Sadly, Kellas himself never saw Everest 'in the flesh'. On one of his reconnaissances he had sent on a couple of the Sherpas to take photographs, which Kellas felt were of Everest; when the 1921 expedition reached Rongbuk for the first time, they found out that he was right. After Darjeeling the party walked through Sikkim and into Tibet. Mallory gives us a description of Kellas, to whom he instantly took a liking. 'Kellas I love already. He is beyond description Scotch and uncouth in his speech – altogether uncouth.' Clearly, despite all his years far from home Kellas had not lost his native Doric brogue! Mallory also describes Kellas' unusual physical appearance, of which he was apparently careless:

> He arrived…very dishevelled, having walked in from Grom, a little place four miles away. His appearance would form an admirable model to the stage for a farcical representation of an alchemist. He is very slight in build, short, thin, stooping and narrow-chested; his head made grotesque by veritable gig-lamps of spectacles and a long pointed moustache. He is an absolutely devoted and disinterested person.

'Genuine and unselfish' was another verdict passed on Kellas. This was in notable contrast to the other Scot on the expedition, Harold Raeburn, a man who often climbed in collar and tie and was very particular. A hugely famous mountaineer, Raeburn was by this time 56, crusty and as universally unpopular as Kellas was popular. Mallory observes that 'Raeburn says he does not expect to go higher than 24,000ft. Dr Kellas presumably will get no further.' Kellas, at 53, and Raeburn were considered veterans in the party, and indeed they both soon fell ill with dysentery, due to the poor and unhygienic food. Raeburn was invalided out: his health was broken and he ended his life in 1926 in an Edinburgh mental hospital. Kellas' fate was to be swifter. Chronic dysentery weakened him and induced heart failure. It is clear now that Kellas had overstrained himself, returning from exploration work to join the expedition of 1921. Mallory describes the agony of Kellas, suffering from an ailment that in those days would be seen as humiliating:

> The old gentleman (such he seemed) was obliged to retire a number of times en route and could not bear to be seen in this distress, and insisted that everyone should be in front of him

Mallory adds, 'He died without one of us anywhere near him,' on 5 June 1921. Kellas was buried at a place called Kampa Dzong, with the peaks of Sikkim that he had climbed visible to the south. Mallory wrote to Geoffrey Winthrop Young:

> It was an extraordinarily affecting little ceremony burying Kellas on a stony hillside – a place on the edge of a great plain and looking across it to the three great snow peaks of his conquest. I shan't easily forget the four boys, his own trained mountain men, children of nature [the Sherpas] seated in wonder on a great stone near the grave while Bury read out the passage from Corinthians.

Sadly, according to Mallory, it was on the day after burying Kellas that the expedition caught their first sight of Everest. After only a climb of 1,000ft from Kampa Dzong the team 'saw what we came to see' in Mallory's words; the Mother Goddess of the World, which Kellas himself had only seen in a partial photograph. *The Times* ran an obituary on Kellas, calling Kampa Dzong 'a fitting resting place for a great mountaineer'. The highest point climbed on the expedition of 1921 itself was 22,500ft and Mallory wished to name a local mountain Mt Kellas in honour of the man he knew so briefly and so admired. Ironically, despite the insistence on Mount Everest as the 'proper' name for Chomolungma, this was vetoed by the secretary of the Everest Committee, Hinks, who stated, 'He [Mallory] must not keep calling mountains by personal names, for they certainly will not be allowed to stick. The idea is enough to make poor Kellas turn in his grave at Kampa Dzong.'

Kellas did not carry out his oxygen experiments in 1921 and the debate about the gas continued to rage. But now we know that Kellas' belief that a fit acclimatised person could climb Everest without oxygen, is correct. Kellas also believed in small expeditions, which had predominated up to this time. In the 1930s these were generally replaced by the huge military-style operations of the kind which were eventually to achieve success in 1953. But many criticised this trend and paid tribute to Kellas. One such was Eric Shipton who in *Upon that Mountain* argued that, 'The sad thing was that the lessons taught by the great pioneers of Himalayan exploration – Longstaff, Conway, Kellas, Godwin-Austen, Freshfield, the Schlagintweits – who achieved so much by the simple and hardy application of their art, were forgotten or ignored.'

Kellas would be pleased that the trend has swung back to smaller, Alpine-style Himalayan expeditions in the last decades. Mallory and Shipton, both giants of Himalayan mountaineering, combined to sing the praises of Kellas. Surely it is time for him to be better known in his own country?

In 2011 Luath Press published a full-scale biography of Alexander Kellas by Ian R Mitchell and George Rodway, entitled *Prelude to Everest*.

Note

1 Tom Patey, Aberdeen's greatest mountaineer after Kellas, was not free of a certain parochialism as well, as witnessed in the ditty from *One Man's Mountains*:

Masherbrum, Gasherbrum, Distegal Sar
They're very good training for Dark Lochnagar.

I myself recall my residual North East pride being recently hurt when the eminent Canadian mountaineer Chic Scott said to me, 'Forget that Parallel B and Craig Meaghaidh Crab Crawl shit, Ian, what Patey did was Mustagh Tower and Rakaposhi.' But is that how he is seen in the North East, or how he saw himself? *I hae ma doots.*

CHAPTER ELEVEN

The Names on the Slugain Howff Memorial: The Dreamers of Beinn a' Bhuird

WITH THE CAIRNGORM CLUB'S foundation in the 1880s, Aberdeen was in the van of the Victorian movement of the middle and upper classes onto the Scottish mountains. And when it came to the 20th century Proletarian Revolution and the invasion of the hills by members of the working classes, the city was not far behind. In Glasgow people like Jock Nimlin and the Creag Dhu were emerging to prominence in the 1930s, following less well-known proletarian pioneers in the 1920s. They were followed in Dundee by Sid Scroggie and others of the superior artisanry who were in evidence on the bens before World War Two. The Aberdeen scene still remained dominated by a fairly traditional Cairngorm Club whose activities were largely limited to walking, rather than rock climbing. But before 1939 the Etchachan Club was founded, amongst whose members were Mac Smith (see below) and other more demotic elements.

Before 1945 there were few climbing routes of character in the Cairngorms, other than Eagle's Ridge on Lochnagar and the Cumming-Crofton route on Beinn a' Bhuird. Local climbing in Tom Patey's words 'had not gone beyond the gully epoch'. Consider: there was a Scottish Mountaineering Club *Guide to Ben Nevis* before World War Two, but the first volume of the *Cairngorms Area* guidebook did not appear till 1961. Amongst the names of those responsible for the post-war explosion were Patey himself, and others such as Bill Brooker, both of whom wrote about their activities, especially Patey, whose articles were collected in *One Man's Mountains*, published in 1971. But there were others involved who were less well-known, even locally.

Because they were part of Aberdeen's mountaineering Proletarian Revolution, they tended to simply record their achievements and not write about them in articles and books – which is the main path to immortality.

To me they were only names. Names of the notifications of first ascents in the *Cairngorms Area* guidebook, or rattled out in the superb chapter 'Cairngorm Commentary' in Patey's book:

> Even the names by which they were known invited a wealth of conjecture – Sandy-Sandy, Ashy, Chesty, Dizzie, Sticker, Esposito...There was Charlie Smith...whistling some obscure aria; Mac Smith and Kenny Winram arguing about the early New Orleans trumpeters, Jamie Robertson engrossed in Marx; Freddy and Sticker the inseparables, plotting new routes in Coire na Ciche...Chesty Bruce, resplendent in tartan shirt and wide toothy grin...

I came onto the hills in the mid-1960s, a decade and a half later than these characters, and at that time had no acquaintance with Freddy Malcolm, Chesty Bruce, Ashie Brebner or the others. About a third of a century later luck favoured me with belated contact and I was able to hear some of their stories; stories of the working class underbelly of Cairngorm climbing, of the self-taught tigers and mountain dreamers...

As usual serendipity played a part in putting faces to the names. In the later 1980s I co-authored a book, *Mountain Days and Bothy Nights*, which contained a chapter on the fabled Secret Howff of Beinn a' Bhuird – without, naturally, revealing its location. I had attributed its building to a certain Freddy Malcolm, because that is what Tom Patey says in his book and because that was also the accepted oral tradition in my teens – and you don't question the *cognoscenti* at that age. More than a decade after the book's publication I got a letter from Ashie Brebner, saying that he was delighted to hear that the howff still existed, the more so as he and his pals had built it almost half a century ago. He added that Freddy Malcolm's howff was another such in the area, built slightly before his own and now in ruins. Ashie's methodology brooked no opposition: who could dispute something dated and remembered by a severe hangover?

Here is Ashie's (edited) account, the full letter having been reprinted in the SMCJ (1999):

> Six of us were involved. Jim Robertson, a stone mason; Charlie Smith, a diver with the harbour board (in the days of diving suits with steel helmets); Doug Mollison who worked in the Town House; Jack Dovery, a steel erector; Jack Innes, a dental mechanic, and myself, Ashie Brebner...
>
> We were being harried by the gamekeepers all the time, but they never came into that gully. We spent the whole autumn of 1952 building the walls choosing the right stones from the nearby scree. We came across a few hibernating adders I remember. At that time most of us had to work on a Saturday morning... it must have been February or March 1953 that we were ready for the heavy materials to come in... mostly timbers and a tarpaulin, a temporary roof till the corrugated iron could be smuggled in... One of the brewers had taken out a special Coronation Ale, which was pretty potent stuff, and by the time the bus arrived we could hardly stand up...The conductress was almost rolling on the floor at our antics in trying to get all the bits and pieces through the narrow bus door...We staggered off the bus in total darkness, clambering over the fallen trunks and branches [note: from the Great Gale of 1953) and within a few yards each of us was completely disoriented.
>
> We woke up at first light to discover that we were in full view of the big house [this was Invercauld, home of the laird Farquharson] and got up in a panic, gathered our materials and set off in search of the others. We found Doug Mollison. He was lying upside down, rucksack still on and fast asleep with his legs draped over a tree trunk. We roused him and located the others and [got] past all the houses as quickly as possible.
>
> The building work went very well. The only one with any building experience was Jim Robertson. He had taken all his

stonemason's tools and acted as a foreman giving each of us a job to do. Over the course of the next few weeks we kept a tighter control of the Coronation Ale and managed to get in all the corrugated iron, and by the spring it was all complete.

We were all mad about Italian Opera and before the days of transistors Charlie would have miles of aerial trailing everywhere, twiddle the knobs in a tiny radio and with earphones in a billy-can we could all hear opera broadcast directly from Milan. That was a great experience at that time.

Ashie remembered Kenny Winram and Mac (Malcolm) Smith as the duo who constructed a much more rudimentary howff than the Slugain one. It was high on the mountain from which they took part in the first ascent of Tantalus Gully in Coire an Dubh Lochain with GC Grieg in 1953, and whence they also did the first ascent off

Inside Slugain Howff
Rita Malcolm cooking on a primus stove inside the howff in the 1950s, in period attire. The KEEP LEFT sign was still there in the 1960s, and we ascribed a political significance to it.

Laminated Crag in Garbh Choire in the same year. Mac Smith, after wartime military service, became a joiner in Hall Russell's shipyard in Aberdeen, and was a self-taught entomologist, who Ashie recalls later fulfilled his dreams by working with the Nature Conservancy. I have a letter from Switzerland from a man who met Mac Smith on an osprey watch whilst Mac was still working in the shipyards, and he describes his amazement at the encounter, 'I shared a tent with Mac. I remember him as a kindly, modest man who told me he was a joiner. And there he was reading Emile Zola's *Germinal* and a Penguin book on ants. That made a deep impression on me. Burns' "Man of independent mind".'

Mac Smith also wrote the second volume of the original SMC *Cairngorms Guide* in 1962. Others were cut short in their dreaming. Kenny Winram later had a very bad fall on Lochnagar and Jim Robertson, the stonemason and artisan/architect of the Slugain Howff – whom Patey in his book recalls as being always 'engrossed in Marx' – died in the Asian flu epidemic of 1957.

Ashie recently wrote to me that,

> The single most important thing which allowed working class youngsters to get into the hills was the availability of ex-army equipment. In the years following the war... a commando framed rucksack made of rubber-backed fabric could be bought for about five shillings and an ice axe for two shillings and sixpence...
>
> I arrived on the scene in 1949/50. Others who appeared to be much older had been going out in the Strachan's bus since being demobbed after the war... You arrived at Bon Accord Square for the 3.15 bus on a Saturday. It was a case of going around all the little groups of climbers to discover where they hoped to go that weekend... Newcomers were generally welcomed and invited to join a particular group. Incidentally I cannot recall maps being used very often. Those older than we appeared very knowledgeable and confident and we would happily follow them into new territory.

This pattern, of (usually) skilled working men escaping onto the hills, finding a series of new horizons, and thus feeding a discontent with proletarian existence and a search for something else, is a familiar one. And for a while in the more fluid post-war society, many were able to achieve such dreams. (In the 1960s the group I went around with contained engineers, a car mechanic, a shipyard worker and an unskilled factory worker, many of who went on from the mountains to university education.) Ashie himself is a good example of this from the previous decade. After working for many years in Pirie Appleton's envelope factory, where many of his relatives were also employed, he quit his job and in the early 1960s set up a small guiding business in the Highlands. With the wood-carving skills he also developed, he was able to remain fully occupied in the outdoors till his retirement. Of Freddy Malcolm, Ashie knew nothing, not having seen him – or indeed any other of his 1950s companions – for almost 40 years. Ashie doubted if Freddy would even remember him.

But he did.

'*That wis the loon fa hid bells on his boots,*' said Freddy, recalling a youthful eccentricity that Ashie later confessed to me. I had heard at that time that Freddy had come back to Aberdeen about 25 years before, just about the time I left the city myself, attracted by the opportunity of work in the oil boom that was starting. Luckily one of my old friends in Aberdeen, who knew I was looking into the question of Freddy and the Dreamers of Beinn a' Bhuird, wrote and asked me if I wanted to meet him, as my pal was working with him offshore. They were both making their living (as many Aberdeen climbers did from the 1970s onwards) doing inspection and safety work abseiling from the oil platforms. Whilst the dole supported many of the climbing fraternity in the rest of the UK in the 1980s, seasonal work on the oil rigs supported many of the same group in Aberdeen. 'Ask if he wants to talk to me,' I cautiously suggested (some do, some don't), and the call came and was followed by a couple of long chats up in Furryboots Toun itself.

Unlike Ashie and many of the others under discussion here, Freddy had remained a manual worker all his life. A welder to trade, after National Service he worked in the Sheffield steel industry till the oil boom allowed him to return to Aberdeen, and he worked there till his retirement, after which he did some post-retirement work abseiling on hydro-dams doing safety checks, and started the task of completing his Munros. He was still full of enthusiasm and very fit when I met him, still climbing at a good standard. Most of his new routes however were done in a fit of activity in the 1950s, much of it from the base of his now ruinous howff, built with his main partner Alex 'Sticker' Thom. They formed a small and short-lived club called

Freddy and the Dreamers
Freddy Malcolm, Sticker Thom and another on Bheinn a' Bhuird in the 1950s.
Gear and clothing were much the same in the 1960s. Much of it was
ex-Army equipment.

the Kincorth Club (after the housing estate where many of them lived and where I myself grew up), a club which even managed to produce one issue of a journal before its dispersal.

As a youngster Freddy would sit in the back of the return bus from Braemar to Aberdeen on a Sunday and listen to the old hands talking about 'new routes'. He decided that he would do some. The only guide book he had was Alexander's pre-war *Cairngorms Guide*, reprinted in 1950. In it Alexander referred to 'the unclimbed Hourglass Buttress, so named for its shape... On Coire na Ciche in Beinn a' Bhuird.' Without further knowledge and with little preparation or experience, Freddy and his accomplices decided to climb it. And between 1953 and '55 they put up the Severe or Very Severe routes of Trident, The Carpet and Hourglass Buttress itself, described in the 1965 *'Gorms Guide* as 'the best and hardest route in Coire na Ciche and one of the best in the massif'. Patey in his own book comments that 'Coire na Ciche came to be regarded as [Kincorth] Club property'.

Here Patey resigns himself to a situation that had originally caused a furore in the small world of North East climbing. He and Bill Brooker had had their eyes on Hourglass Buttress, only to have it snatched from them by a couple of unknown whippersnappers. A few days after the climb Freddy found Patey on his doorstep, demanding details of the route and adding that he and Brooker regarded it as having been nicked from them. This rivalry was good natured though, and Freddy and Sticker later climbed with Tom Patey, putting up for example Sabre Cut on Creag an Dubh Loch in 1957, a Grade 4. All these climbs were done in tricounis, in an area where vibram and crampons even had made little headway at that time. Freddy does admit that Aberdonian meanness, in not wanting to abandon any nailed boots till they were totally worn out, might have had something to do with such conservatism.

A modest guy, Freddy expressed the opinion that there would be *'nae much tae write aboot'* concerning his exploits. But he and the others who dreamed their dreams on Beinn a' Bhuird 50 or more years ago deserve to have their activities and achievements recognised, and a forthcoming history of Cairngorm climbing will doubtless do them justice[1]. Recognition came to the builders of the howff when, in a poignant ceremony, I accompanied Ashie, the last alive of the six who built it, to Slugain to install a memorial plaque he had made to commemorate the half century of the Secret Howff's existence. All the Dreamers had taken journeys which, whilst not getting them as far from home as Kellas' expeditions, had been equally worthwhile and fulfilling.

And here is a wee story for you. Emigration was one of the dreams of improvement of working men in the 1950s. Both Sticker Thom and Chesty Bruce emigrated to Canada and lived relatively close to each other in the Rocky Mountains of Alberta – without being aware of this. Freddy Malcolm had kept up contact with Sticker and the pair was descending a mountain in the Rockies one day when an ascending mountaineer betrayed by his brogue that he was from the Granite City; it was Chesty, and contacts were renewed. And by that similar serendipity of the mountaineering community which is actually a function of its smallness, a mere year or so after getting to know Ashie, I was in Canada talking about Scotland's

THE NAMES ON THE SLUGAN HOWFF MEMORIAL: THE DREAMERS OF BEINN A' BHUIRD

mountains – and in the audience was Chesty, who had climbed with Ashie 40 years before. By a happy chance another contact was reforged when I put Chesty and Ashie back in touch.

And Aberdonian working class climbing has outlasted the demise of the Proletarian Revolution tradition elsewhere, partly through the emergence of the oil industry. Long after the Scottish mountains elsewhere had again become a largely middle class preserve, horny-handed sons of toil from Furryboots Toun were still conspicuous on the bens – or at least in the Cairngorm ones. But that is not my story to tell.

Note

1   Between writing this and its going to print appeared the massively researched work by Greg Strange, *The Cairngorms* (2010), where Freddy and the others have their achievements recognised.

Some other books published by **LUATH** PRESS

Clydeside: Red, Orange and Green

Ian R Mitchell
ISBN 1 906307 70 9 PBK £9.99

There's more to Clydeside than Glasgow. The River Clyde links west of Scotland communities shaped by a potent mix of Red Clydeside radicalism and Green and Orange religious loyalties.

Ian R Mitchell takes you on a journey along the River Clyde and shows it's not just about the remnants of shipbuilding, relating stories of conflicts, people and communities. The river rolls from Lanarkshire upriver, once renowned for its coal and steel production, to former centres of textile production such as Paisley and the Vale of Leven, with many other places equally rich in industrial history along its 100 mile course. From Robert Owen's New Lanark utopian experiment to the Little Moscow of the Vale of Leven, here is a working class history rich in political and industrial innovation.

Ian Mitchell's infectious enthusiasm for the places visited in this book leaves the reader with a compelling urge to don walking shoes and retrace his steps.
THE MORNING STAR

This City Now: Glasgow and its working class past

Ian R Mitchell
ISBN 1 84282 082 6 PBK £12.99

This City Now sets out to retrieve the hidden architectural, cultural and historical riches of some of Glasgow's working class districts. Many who enjoy the fruits of Glasgow's recent gentrification will be surprised and delighted by the gems which Ian Mitchell has uncovered beyond the usual haunts.

An enthusiastic walker and historian, Mitchell invites us to recapture the social and political history of the working class in Glasgow, by taking us on a journey from Partick to Rutherglen, and Clydebank to Pollokshaws, revealing the buildings which go unnoticed every day yet are worthy of so much more attention.

Once read and inspired, you will never be able to walk through Glasgow in the same way again.

...both visitors and locals can gain instruction and pleasure from this fine volume... Mitchell is a knowledgable, witty and affable guide through the streets of the city...
GREEN LEFT WEEKLY

Mountain Days & Bothy Nights

Dave Brown & Ian R Mitchell

ISBN 1 906307 83 0 PBK £7.50

'One thing we'll pit intae it is that there's mair tae it than trudging up and doon daft wet hills.'

This classic 'bothy book' celebrates everything there is to hillwalking; the people who do it, the stories they tell and the places they sleep. Where bothies came from, the legendary walkers, the mountain craftsmen and the Goretex and gaiters brigade – and the best and the worst of the dosses, howffs and bothies of the Scottish hills.

On its 21st anniversary, the book that tried to show the camaraderie and buccaneering spirit of Scottish hillwalking in the early days has now become part of the legends of the hills. Still likely to inspire you to get out there with a sleeping bag and a hipflask, this new edition brings a bit of mountaineering history to the modern Munro bagger. The climbers dossing down under the corries of Lochnagar may have changed in dress, politics and equipment, but the mountains and the stories are timeless.

Dave Brown and Ian R Mitchell won the Boardman-Tasker Prize for Mountain Literature in 1991 for *A View from the Ridge*, the sequel to *Mountain Days & Bothy Nights*.

A View from the Ridge

Dave Brown and Ian R Mitchell

ISBN 1 905222 45 9 PBK £7.50

Winner of Boardman-Tasker Prize for Mountain Literature

To some, hillwalking is a physical activity. To others, climbing is all, and everything else is nothing. Because it's not just hills: it's people, characters, fun and tragedy. Every mountaineer will know that it's not just about the anticipation of what hill to climb next, it's a sub-culture of adventure and friendship – all-night card games, monumental hangovers, storytelling, singing – and above all, free spirits.

In this fitting sequel and essential companion to the classic *Mountain Days & Bothy Nights*, Dave Brown and Ian R Mitchell capture perfectly the inexplicable desire which brings Scottish hillwalkers back to the mist, mud and midgies every weekend. Their lively, humorous and enthusiastic narrative will revitalise the drive in you to get out on the hills – or you may prefer just to curl up on the couch with this book and a wee dram for company.

If you buy only one mountain book this year make it this 'view from the ridge' and savour its rich, different and fascinating reflections.

KEVIN BORMAN
High Mountain Magazine

Details of these and other books published by Luath Press can be found at:
www.luath.co.uk

Luath Press Limited
committed to publishing well written books worth reading

LUATH PRESS takes its name from Robert Burns, whose little collie Luath (*Gael.*, swift or nimble) tripped up Jean Armour at a wedding and gave him the chance to speak to the woman who was to be his wife and the abiding love of his life. Burns called one of 'The Twa Dogs' Luath after Cuchullin's hunting dog in Ossian's *Fingal*. Luath Press was established in 1981 in the heart of Burns country, and is now based a few steps up the road from Burns' first lodgings on Edinburgh's Royal Mile.
Luath offers you distinctive writing with a hint of unexpected pleasures.

Most bookshops in the UK, the US, Canada, Australia, New Zealand and parts of Europe either carry our books in stock or can order them for you. To order direct from us, please send a £sterling cheque, postal order, international money order or your credit card details (number, address of cardholder and expiry date) to us at the address below. Please add post and packing as follows: UK – £1.00 per delivery address; overseas surface mail – £2.50 per delivery address; overseas air-mail – £3.50 for the first book to each delivery address, plus £1.00 for each addition-al book by airmail to the same address. If your order is a gift, we will happily enclose your card or message at no extra charge.

Luath Press Limited
543/2 Castlehill
The Royal Mile
Edinburgh EH1 2ND
Scotland
Telephone: 0131 225 4326 (24 hours)
Fax: 0131 225 4324
email: sales@luath.co.uk
Website: www.luath.co.uk